Dear Joey

*May you enjoy my
adventure + continue
to build yours.*

Sam

LOST
— and —
FOUND
...

Seeking the Past and Finding Myself

SAM THIARA

GNITE THE DREAM

Cataloguing in publication information is available from
Library and Archives Canada.
ISBN 978-0-9937581-5-7 (paperback)
ISBN 978-0-9937581-6-4 (ebook)

Some names and identifying details have been changed to
protect the privacy of individuals.

Produced by Page Two
www.pagetwo.com

Cover design by Jennifer Lum
Interior design by Setareh Ashrafologhalai
Interior photos by Sam Thiara

sam-thiara.com

CONTENTS

*Going on a journey makes you stronger,
resilient, and better able to appreciate who you are.
This book is dedicated to everyone on a journey.*

Travel isn't always pretty. It isn't always comfortable. Sometimes it hurts, it even breaks your heart. But that's okay. The journey changes you; it should change you. It leaves marks on your memory, on your consciousness, on your heart, and on your body. You take something with you. Hopefully, you leave something good behind.

ANTHONY BOURDAIN

PROLOGUE

SOME OF THE world's greatest treasures cannot be bought, and might even be called simple, common, or plain by some. My treasure was purchased by overcoming obstacles and not listening to the noise.

This book started as a way to share my adventure of travelling to India for the first time to seek out my ancestral roots. Something inside me wanted to learn about my origins and the distant place where my ancestors had come from. I needed to learn about things that were being forgotten.

Armed with just a faded photograph and very little information, my wife and I embarked on a trip to India, unsure what we would experience and uncover. The odds were certainly against me, because there was very little sound information to accompany the photo. Our three-week trip proved to be a small window of time. As our adventure was coming to a close, I had to act fast. There were just hours left before this door to my past was going to close, but I hadn't come this far simply to turn around and go home without my treasure.

What I did not realize was that the earlier part of my trip to find my ancestral roots would shake my foundations; eventually, I discovered that I was searching for my personal identity. Unfortunately, we get busy with our lives and sometimes pave over the important questions, such as "Where do I come from?" or "Who was here before me?" Slowly, as I wrote and thought more about my trip to India, I realized that this journey to discover my family roots was also a journey to find myself, my own roots. When I was growing up, Canadians saw me as Indian, yet Indians saw me as Canadian—I was not sure who I was in those terms.

For some readers, my story might be an interesting travel adventure. For others, my words could raise questions about their own identity. Some may find comfort and hope that they can realize their personal search to connect with their past. Others might look to the voyage as inspiration that they can do anything they set out to do, despite the odds that may be against them. For all of you, I hope you find what you're looking for in these pages, or that my words send you on your own journey of discovery.

1

HEADING
SOMEWHERE

A REALIZATION HIT ME at 33,000 feet: I was a foreigner heading to a country that should not be foreign to me. With the seconds ticking away during my flight to India, an uneasiness engulfed me as I got closer and closer to embarking on my search for my ancestral roots. I felt so distant from this place, a country I'd never visited. There was nothing familiar about India except the images I held, which had been based on the few Bollywood films I had seen and on the times I'd sat in temples waiting impatiently for the religious service to end. The word "uncertainty" sat prominently in my mind.

Physically, my appearance is Indian, but looks are deceiving. I struggle with my identity as a British-born

Indian who has lived in Canada for most of his life, and whose parents came from Fiji. So am I even Indian? Am I Canadian? Who am I? I stared into the darkness and the outline of the seat in front of me and pondered these thoughts as I shifted around in the economy-class seat. All I knew was that I was racing towards a destination like no other I had been to, not fully confident that I was prepared for what was about to consume me.

The initial idea for this journey was not about finding myself, but about seeking out my paternal grandfather's house, our roots. The family tree was bare because a couple of generations had passed and so had the knowledge of, and connection with, our relations in India. I needed to meet this challenge head-on, and it was going to be quite difficult because no one seemed to know where our village was. Forget trying to find a needle in a haystack; I was not even clear on where the haystack was!

I flicked the light on and looked at my wife, Sadhna, sleeping in the seat next to me. I glanced at my watch and realized we had been in the air or in terminals for more than twelve hours. We were now somewhere over the Atlantic Ocean. The feeling at this point was that time was standing still, and I was already tired and anxious to land. But we really did not know anyone in India. What if the car and driver we had booked were not there? How would we make it to the hotel? I had read and had been told horror stories of taxi drivers taking unsuspecting passengers to far-off places and then only delivering them to their hotel if they paid a bribe.

I glanced at Sadhna again and was amazed at how easily she curls up into a ball and falls asleep on a flight.

She'd nodded off as soon as we were in the air. I guess that is quite possible when you're five foot two. At six feet tall, I don't think I could ever form myself into a ball on a seat and be comfortable. My knees continually grazed the back of the seat in front of me, a constant reminder of how tight the space was. I looked around and saw that most people had fallen asleep, but there were a few lights dotted around the cabin, like the stars outside, highlighting the restless travellers like me.

I was not interested in watching the in-flight movie. I also did not feel like reading, so I pulled out my travel book and opened it to the map of India. Having Indian roots, I should have no problems there, right? I could speak Hindi to a certain degree, and my wife speaks it fluently. Prior to this trip, I had taken a course in Punjabi to become a bit more fluent in that language. As I questioned myself again about my knowledge of the country we were about to visit, I felt I appreciated and understood the mainstream cultural aspects, such as the various religions, and had a firm grasp of the modern-day history. I believed I should be fine. At this point you consider the research you have done, the books you have read, the people you have spoken to, and you think you are ready, like an athlete who has dedicated their time to training.

As I looked at the map, there were three key things that I told myself I must do while in India. The first was to see one of the most photographed and visited sites in the world, the Taj Mahal. Was it really as beautiful as they say? The second was to visit the Golden Temple at Amritsar in Punjab, considered the holiest place for

Sikhs. I needed to experience this because, being Sikh myself, this was part of my ancestral roots and would allow me to pay my respects to generations gone. The third, and probably the most challenging, was to seek out and find my paternal grandfather's house. I had decided on this journey a year earlier. Something was drawing me to seek out my foundations and roots, and was now pulling me to India at about 885 kilometres per hour.

The challenge when it came to finding my grandfather's house was that I had only a faded photograph and very little information on what this village was called and where it was located. My father's older brother had taken the photograph decades ago, but he had passed away before we could gather the relevant information. My cousin in California, my uncle's son, sent it to me as a link to our past just two days before Sadhna and I left on our trip. The photo showed four adults and four children in the front and a few people in the back. I knew the name of the village as Chodauri. The post office where my father sent letters, on behalf of my grandfather, was Garhshankar and the district was Hoshiarpur. It should be easy enough to find, and with my finger I traced along the small map, the northern region of India called the Punjab, and looked at where part of my journey was going to take me. It was a huge region and I was not sure I was fully prepared.

I have always appreciated a challenge, and this one was substantial. With a confident voice, I have repeatedly said, "I thrive in uncertainty and ambiguity," and there was no shortage of either of those themes in this

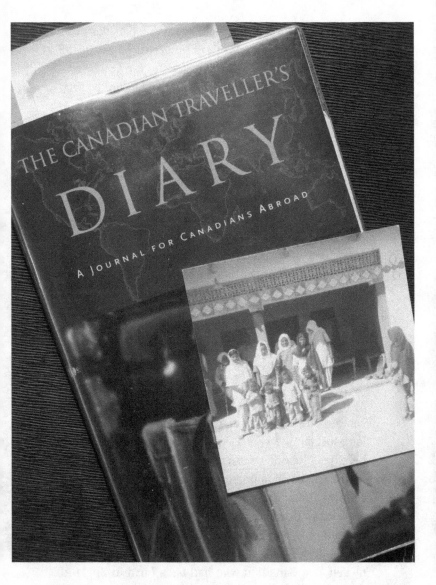

My journey began with a photograph and a journal.

situation. As a result, sitting there in the semi-darkness, I thought, *I do not want this to be as easy as getting off the plane, getting into a car, driving for hours, and knowing where this village is. It has to be challenging! To not attempt is a far greater risk than sitting back and thinking of what might have been. If I don't try, then I have only shadows of what might have been, and that is not good enough for me.*

I took out the old photograph and studied it. The image was about three and a half inches square and had an orange tinge to it. It was about thirty-five years old. It showed a few adults and children, standing, dressed in traditional northern Indian outfits, and seated in the back was an older gentleman. I could barely make out their faces. I stared at the image and wondered who they were and if they were still around. I had based everything on such limited information, and my thoughts were conflicted. It was like building a jigsaw puzzle with only some of the pieces and no picture on the lid to reference. Was this journey to find my village a ridiculous adventure? Was I foolish even to try? But if, by some remote chance, I happened upon the village and my long-lost family, what a significant discovery that would be. Since the odds were against me, I decided to look on the trip as an opportunity to experience in person a country I had only read about.

I thought back to my life growing up in Canada. For a number of years I had rebelled and pushed away my Indian identity because I wanted to fit in. I thought of myself as a Canadian who had been born in England, with some level of roots going back to the Fiji islands, and somewhere in the mix was India. For much of my younger life, I pushed down the physical traits that singled me out as "different," as well as my cultural identity. It was only later, in my university days, that I started to gain more of an appreciation for my Indian roots. Perhaps I was maturing and realizing there is a benefit to having a diverse background. Instead of walking on one side of the line or the other, maybe I could have a comfortable stance on both sides.

People wonder why the search mattered to me so much. Could I not be satisfied with just enjoying India? There were two driving forces on why this was important to me. First, if I didn't seek out this village, and if this knowledge skipped another generation, our village would be lost to us forever. Right now, any hope of finding the village was connected to me by the thinnest of threads.

Second, my father, who has done so much for us as a family, became a paraplegic after an industrial accident in 1972. He had never been to India and would never venture there, so I wanted to do something meaningful for him: find our village and his father's birthplace. I knew that my setting foot in our ancestral home would mean a lot to him and our extended family.

As I stared at the map, excitement and concern filled my mind. The more I thought about where I was headed, the more impossible it seemed that I would be able to sleep. I put the picture and map away and turned off my light. I looked around at everyone in the shadows of the plane. Some were going home, some were going to visit family, and others were travelling for business. Each was on a journey.

I sat there and listened to the humming of the plane's engines. *Only six and a half hours to go... Boy, is this going to be one long, drawn-out flight.* I put my head-phones on and closed my eyes. I thought of my father, my uncles and aunts, and the grandfather I had never really known.

Every so often I would open my eyes and check my watch. The minutes stretched painfully into hours. I shifted in my seat once more, trying to find a comfortable position. I reclined my seat ever so slowly so it wouldn't startle the person behind me. I took a deep breath as I closed my eyes and tried to force myself to sleep. The spa music in my headphones, mixed with the dull sound of the engine, helped me to slip into a semi-sleep.

2

LEARNING
ABOUT MY
GRANDFATHER

IN ORDER TO move forward, one must first uncover the past. By knowing about my grandfather, you might better appreciate the journey I undertook to assemble a family puzzle.

Labh Singh was my paternal grandfather. Phuman Singh was my maternal grandfather. I will focus on Labh Singh in this story, as it was his house and village that I was looking for. But equally, I want to pay my respects here to my grandfather Phuman Singh. I mention him as he was also a very respectable man, serving in the First World War and leading an honourable life in Fiji.

I did not get to know my grandfather Labh very well. To me, he is only shadows and stories. At three years old, everyone seemed tall to me. He wore a white turban that was neatly tied, had a round face, and did not speak much. He had a caring but stoic look, and a stout build—he seemed solid. His piercing eyes were softened by a neatly trimmed white moustache, but I don't remember his other features.

I left England with my family when I was almost four and we went to settle in Vancouver, so I only knew him for that length of time. The first time I went back to England was with my family when I was just over six years old. A few months earlier, he'd passed away at my aunt and uncle's house in Southampton.

We landed in London on a cold morning, and were picked up by relatives and driven to Southampton. I recall being reconnected with family, but I was more interested in hanging out with my cousins than learning about my roots. I knew only that Labh was my grandfather and we had recently lost him, and that my parents were sad. It is only through looking at old and creased photos that I can start to piece this person together. Learning about him, his journey, and our village came much later in life.

Since I never really got to know my grandfather, I had to ask around and learn about him through the memories of others. My father, uncles, and aunts were able to share some aspects of his life with me over the years. Memories have to be activated when they are left for a long time and not tended to, and when you sit and ask questions, you get smiles and looks into space as the other person recalls stories of their own upbringing. They think back to their childhood and are enveloped in the company of those people who no longer exist. What started out as me asking a few questions resulted in a flood of memories, stories, and laughter. The experiences might have happened a long time ago, but they still served up vivid sights, sounds, and flavours. As my relatives shared, they tried to fill in voids that were difficult for me to appreciate. I could only grasp some ideas and thoughts to try to satisfy my own curiosity. My father relived his childhood memories when I asked him what his father was like as a person. I learned about my father's mischief and antics growing up. Sometimes a memory would start off being about my grandfather, but the richness of the conversation then shifted to the speaker's own memories of growing up, which are equally important to capture.

While I sat in the company of my elders, the spark of a comment about me wanting to find the village in India ignited the embers of memories. Before long, these elders were animated and sharing with each other, and I was absorbing it all. Phrases like "Remember when..." or "Wait, wait, didn't we..." circulated around the room, and the conversation went on and on. Before you knew it, there was laughter, stories were being piled onto other stories like a stack of firewood, and the conversation was going back and forth. At the end of it all, everyone would say, "That was a good walk down memory lane. We should do this again!"

Labh Singh was born in Hoshiarpur district in the northern state of Punjab in the late 1800s. My grandfather had an older brother, but I do not know if there were other siblings. With Sikhs, if you were not the eldest, your title to land was limited. Oftentimes, the younger males would venture off to join the military or go to faraway countries in search of adventure, and this is why you see Sikhs all around the world.

My father and uncle shared a story with me about my grandfather's schooling, near his village in the Punjab. In those days, education was considered to be secondary to farm labour. When my grandfather went to school, they sat on the ground and wrote on it using their fingers. The earth was their chalkboard. At the end of the day he went home, and when his mother asked him how the day had gone, he replied, "If I stay in school, we write on the ground using our finger and I may not have a finger in the future because it will wear out." Well, that was enough to convince the family to pull him out of there. A son without a finger was not too helpful on a farm.

While his schooling ended there, my understanding is that he was still a very smart man . . . Well, I guess he demonstrated that when he convinced his parents to pull him out of school! My father said that even if his father did not go to school, he still became a savvy businessman who was full of ideas. He also knew the value of education and made sure his own children went to school. Not much else is known about his days in India, given that he was a quiet man who was private about his personal life.

So how does a young man living a village life in the state of Punjab wind up in Fiji? The two places are as different as one could imagine. With village life, everything familiar and stable was within your daily reach. Fiji would not even have been a concept in the mind of a person in the state of Punjab. It is a landlocked region of fertile farmland far from any body of water, with a mix of South Asian cultures and Sikhs. Fiji, by contrast, is surrounded by ocean. If one is to leave Punjab, you must venture out of the immediate area and make your way to a main city to eventually cross a border or hop on a ship. In the late 1800s, when transportation was not so easy, how did a young man even know which way to go? You leave a country that is home and all the people you know, get on a boat destined for a faraway land, and have no way to communicate with the family and friends you've left behind.

FIJI COMPRISES SEVERAL islands in the South Pacific near Australia, a tropical oasis in the Melanesia region. It was inhabited by native Fijians and overseen by Great Britain as a colony. At that time, Fiji was an agricultural area, with sugar cane the primary crop. The British in Fiji decided to bring indentured labour over from India to look after the sugar cane farming. The Indians, most from the states of Uttar Pradesh and Bihar, thrived in this area, and slowly the population of Fijian Indians began to grow; they became farmers, entrepreneurs, and workers. The promises of land and prosperity did not live up to expectations, as the Fijian Indians were under British colonial rule.

So how does a young adult leave village life in the Punjab and wind up thousands of kilometres away on

My father, along with the aunts and uncles in this image, told me stories that gave me the pieces of the puzzle I needed to find our village. My father, Jagjit, is far left, my grandfather, Labh Singh, Uncle Ranjit in the back centre, Auntie Basant in the front centre, grandmother Raj Kaur, sister Kamala and Uncle Kabul.

a remote island paradise? From what has been shared, when Labh was about eighteen or nineteen years old, he received a scolding from his father and decided to leave the village. But instead of running away to another house, village, or city, he chose to leave the country. No one is sure how Labh left the village and made his way to a port at a time when transportation was not as accessible as it is today. All that is known is that under cover of night, he snuck away with his best friend, leaving everything behind.

Now, if he left with his friend, what that suggests to me is that this was more of a planned departure as opposed to a sudden decision to leave home. Perhaps he had been longing to leave the village and was looking for an excuse, so when his father scolded him, that was enough to persuade him. He somehow boarded a boat that was destined for Australia, Fiji, Argentina, and Trinidad. By all accounts, the most reasonable departure point would have been Calcutta. Somehow, Labh had heard that there were great opportunities in Argentina at cattle ranches, so he had decided to head there. In those days, information was transmitted by word of mouth, and you had to take things on trust. Someone must have shared with him the opportunities that lay beyond the village, and he believed them. Steam liner or train were the only ways to really seek adventure, and in his case the obvious option was to leave the country by water. In 1905, the Union Steam Shipping Company of New Zealand offered regular service between Calcutta and Fiji, with Fiji being a stopoff to North and South

America. Again, trying to fit pieces together, I can only assume that this is how he made his way to Fiji.

Well, plans can change when they are made in haste. In this case, the boat left India and headed to Australia, and either my grandfather had friends he left with from the village or he made friends along the way. Either way, there was a small group of them and they stuck together... to a point. The boat arrived in Australia and two of the men decided to jump ship and swim to the docks. My grandfather was asking himself if this might be where he wanted to settle. While Australia was not Argentina, it was still a place far away from his village. While the two men made their plans to jump ship, my grandfather debated, but common sense prevailed and he decided to stay on board. The fact that Labh couldn't swim may have played a large part in his decision. In any event, the ship departed for its next destination—Fiji—with him safely on board.

It anchored in Suva, Fiji's capital. Labh walked onto the pier and decided to make his life in this place. Either he liked something about the country at first glance or he'd simply had enough of ship travel by this point. Maybe he thought this was Argentina, and discovered his Fiji the same way Columbus was searching for India and landed in North America? Remember, he had been landlocked all his life and was maybe not meant for seafaring travels.

Fiji was not the paradise we think of it as today. The beaches were amazing, but my grandfather did not go there to live on a beach. It's difficult when you are in a foreign land. Fiji at the time was a colony, and it was a tiered society. My grandfather was not on the bottom rung, but he was also not at the top; he was just an individual who blended in. The early Sikhs in Fiji were a tightly knit group. Even though they were spread around the islands, they knew of each other. There is comfort in seeing someone familiar, and as a Sikh, you stand out because of that prominent turban. In Fiji, some Sikhs were ex-military, some were business owners looking for their piece of the local economic pie, and some were just like my grandfather, who really had no future in the village and just went there in search of an adventure. It did not matter how you got there; what mattered was this familiarity that brought them together as a community.

What is known is that he first settled in Taveuni, the third-largest island in Fiji. No one is really sure how and why he settled there rather than on the mainland. He married and had three daughters. Eventually, when he left Taveuni, my grandfather settled in Ba, on the northwest side of the main island, Viti Levu. One of the shortest town names I have ever encountered, Ba lies along the coast, in a drier part of the country. After his first marriage ended, he remarried and had five more children—three sons and two daughters. My father was the second-born in this next round.

Around 1922, the first Sikh temple, or gurdwara, was established in Suva, on the other side of the island, and this provided a base and home for the Sikhs. A gurdwara is a home away from home for Sikhs. No matter where in the world you are, a gurdwara is a safe and comfortable place to rest your body, mind, and soul. It is open to all faiths and provides accommodations for the weary traveller, plus traditional vegetarian meals, beautiful hymns and songs, and a community centre where you can find comfort in conversation. When one is far away from home and seeking some familiar surroundings, all that is needed is a gurdwara.

Later, around the early 1930s, a gurdwara was established in Lautoka and Tavua to serve the needs of the large Sikh population on the western side of Fiji, and that is where my grandfather settled.

My grandfather was both a small-time farmer and an entrepreneur. He tried his hand at growing kava crops, selling vegetables at the local market, and making furniture in a joinery shop. Some of this he found came to him naturally, while other aspects of his life were a struggle. He never made it big, and never visited India again, but he did provide for his family.

3

KNOWING
MY
FATHER

M Y FATHER WAS born in Ba in 1935. He had an older brother, Ranjit, a younger brother, Kabul, and two younger sisters, Basant and Kamala. As the middle boy, he was neither the respected eldest nor the adored youngest. When one grows up in a small area with close family, you have to entertain yourself. My father and his younger brother would always share stories of how they got into trouble together, and how their older brother, Ranjit, would have to apologize on their behalf. I always found it interesting that my father would discipline us, but when we brought up the mischievous ways of his past, somehow that was always a different story and he would change the subject.

My father recalled an incident from when he was very young. There was a bus departing, taking a distant family member away. Everyone came out to say their good-byes and wish this relative well. Tears were shed and promises were made to write letters so that they could all stay in touch. There was a sense that these relations were likely never to seen this person again, and with no phone service, letters would have to do. It turns out that the relative was only going to live in the next town, which was an hour away by bus. In the late 1930s in Fiji, as in the late 1800s in India, one stayed put in familiar surroundings.

My father went to a Catholic school but was not religious. He gained a solid education and learned that he was good with his hands. He was always described as a tall and skinny fellow. I think "skinny as a rail" would not be fair to the rail. He went to the tailor to get a pair of trousers made and was told there would be room for only one pocket, not two, in the back. He was totally healthy and had boundless energy, but the family always worried that he was too thin. They tried everything to fatten him up, but nothing seemed to work. While the family ran a few businesses, what he really enjoyed was woodworking and machining, and this would turn out to be his life.

When my father was about twenty-four, he was newly married to my mom and they had a son, my older brother. While my older brother was given the name Sachindra Jeet Singh, it was far easier to just call him Steve. When my father was about twenty-six, he decided that things needed to change. My uncle Kabul had ventured to England a year earlier and was asking my father to join him. At that time, in the early 1960s, Fiji was a British colony and you could get to England without a visa, as a citizen of the Commonwealth.

When my father was considering leaving for England, some said he should not go. His son was less than a year old, and everything comfortable and safe was in Fiji. My grandfather also questioned why my father was relocating, but after all, my grandfather had left India and made his way to Fiji. Opportunities were abroad, and there was a need to venture out. Prior to going to England, my father had never set foot out of Fiji. Today, it would be as simple as booking a flight, but back in the early 1960s airline travel was not as convenient or affordable as it is now.

My father boarded a flight from Nadi, Fiji, to Sydney, Australia, so he could board a ship in Sydney Harbour that would take him to another world. My father shared how his first-ever flight, at a time when air travel was not readily accessible, was unnerving and scary. A few people he knew had flown away and all they ever received back home was a telegram with a few sporadic words to say the person had arrived safely. It was as if they had sailed into the distance, never to be seen again. In my father's eyes, he was not going to be returning to Fiji for a long time, if ever.

He got to Sydney, but he could not really explore the city as the next morning he was boarding a steamer ship, TN *Sydney*. The ship was doing a run between Sydney, Australia, and Genoa, Italy, with stops in between. There were about fifteen people on the liner whom my father knew or quickly forged a friendship with, and they stuck together in close proximity for the month-long journey. As we know, there is safety in numbers, and the common denominator was that they were all Indians from Fiji. While they did not really know each other well, they were all on an adventure together in search of greater opportunities, and they were all destined for London. They occupied the space below deck commonly referred to as steerage. It was all right as comfort goes, but nothing special. It was relaxed, with six people to each room, sleeping in bunk beds. The food was good and varied: toast, ham, eggs, soup, pasta. Life on board was not boring, but nor was it the most exciting of times.

Their first stop was Singapore. They docked for the day and a group of them decided to go ashore and see the city. Fortunately, they met a Sikh security guard, who was ex-military, and he took the time to show them around. After they re-boarded, the next stop was Mumbai, India, for one day. Then it was through the Suez Canal to their final destination, Genoa. When they arrived there, they were pleased to finally be off the ship and able to explore the city. They went to a place that served "hamburgers." The Hindus in the group told the Muslims to not eat the burgers because they were ham. So the Hindus ate the burgers and the Muslims did not, for fear of religious consequences. If only they'd known!

From Genoa, the group boarded a train that took them to Calais, France, where they got on a ferry for Dover. From my perspective, this entire trip sounds like an amazing adventure! To venture by train from

Italy to France sounds romantic. Once in Dover, a train brought them to Waterloo Station in London. There, they said their goodbyes and dispersed throughout England. My father's destination was Southampton, so he boarded the train for Southampton Central. From there, my father hopped into a taxi and made his way to 199 Derby Road in the St. Mary's area of the city. The relatives in England knew my father was arriving but did not know exactly when. No one answered when he rang the doorbell, so the driver took him to a B&B and my father returned the next day and was welcomed by the family. Eight months later, my mother and Steve arrived by steamship from Suva through the Panama Canal and then to Southampton.

It amazes me that my grandfather, who had lived in one country all his life, could pick up his things and make his way halfway around the world to a totally foreign country and do all of this at a time when long-distance travel was not that common. Equally, my father, mother, and brother travelled by ship halfway around the world in the early 1960s; now, long-distance ocean travel is a rare and luxurious mode of transportation.

My father, always quick-witted, shared a humorous story. Before he left for England, he was talking with an uncle who insisted that in England and the West people eat beef, and as a person of faith, he wanted my father to promise he would not eat beef. My father obliged to satisfy this family member. A year later, this uncle made his way to England. He hadn't forgotten my father's promise, and asked him, "You don't eat beef, now that you live in

England, do you?" Without hesitating, my father replied, "Uncle, I hardly eat chicken!" Thereby avoiding the direct question, he did not lie ... because it was true that he hardly ate chicken. Satisfied, the uncle never asked again.

So, for a number of years, we settled in Southampton, England. One of the memories my father shared with me was that when he got to England, he was surprised to see white British people doing manual labour. In Fiji, all the expats were in posh settings of administrative leadership roles, and they had servants doing the manual work. It is difficult for me to grasp how this observation might impact someone growing up in colonial times because I was not familiar with this world.

The skills my father had gained in Fiji proved to be very beneficial in England. He quickly picked up a truck-driving job in Southampton, and before he knew it he was driving around and learning the roads without our modern technological aids. He always told me how complicated the streets were in London, but he never had a mishap. After the truck-driving job, he got a well-paid post as a machinist making doors and windows. His boss appreciated having him around because he was such a good worker.

So, life in England was definitely different from Fiji, but they made things work. I was born at home at 199 Derby Road on June 30, 1962, about a year after my mother had arrived in England. Back in the day, if there were no complications with the first-born, the second-born was to enter the world at home, which is exactly what happened. It was not a big house, but there

TOP   My memories of life in England are limited. Here I am
with my dad.

BOTTOM   Our family just before our journey to Canada.

were three to four families living in close quarters, as everyone was a new arrival. Even the living room was converted into a bedroom for a family. Shortly after my birth, we moved to 42 Derby Road and our own place.

Southampton had shipping docks and was a very blue-collar city. My memories of the St. Mary's neighbourhood are very limited. I do remember my little tricycle and tearing up and down Derby Road with my brother, but all that was about to change.

One day, my father was walking around the High Street area in Southampton when he happened upon a display put up by the Canadian High Commission aimed at persuading British subjects to apply to immigrate to Canada. My father walked in and was greeted warmly. He was offered coffee, biscuits, and Canadian newspapers. As he sat there and sipped the coffee and read the newspapers, he looked around and saw the typical Canadian images: red-coated Royal Canadian Mounted Police on their horses in the Rockies with a beautiful lake behind them, and Indigenous people in traditional dress. My father recalled that in Fiji, when he saw images of Canada, they were always so beautiful.

The employee from the Canadian High Commission asked my father about his life in Fiji and England. As a machinist, my father caught the eye of the High Commission, as this was an in-demand skill. The representative told my father that he should consider applying. They were going to be there for three days, so he should return before they left. With the paperwork in hand, my father left and said he would be back.

He took the application form home. My mom was not impressed. We had just moved to England and now he wanted to move to Canada. She argued that we had just started to build a life in England, with family, and we did not know anyone in Canada. My father replied that he would fill in the form and hand it in, and if they got accepted somehow, then they could decide.

The next morning, my father took the completed form and went back to the temporary Canadian High Commission office. The employee recognized him and took the application form and did a quick look through. He nodded and talked to himself and then asked my father to take the form into another room. There was a different person there, who looked at it, stamped it, and said, "Congratulations, your visa application for Canada has been accepted pending a medical exam."

Now, at this point I think my father was taken aback. His thoughts turned to how he was going to explain to my mother that he was about to drag us all to another country. My father said, "Great! We will leave in six months" (so that he would have time to convince my mother) and the representative said, "How about six weeks?"

After much convincing, my mom finally reluctantly agreed and we were off to Canada. I asked my father why he picked Vancouver out of such a vast country and he gave me two reasons. First, there were only two families in Canada we knew, and they were both in North Vancouver. So that made the choice very easy. The other reason was sentimental, as he knew that Vancouver sat on the west coast and near the Pacific Ocean, and therefore shared the Pacific shores with Fiji. Looking back, I was glad we did not have family in the colder parts of Canada. Vancouver is a beautiful place, but I am sure that if he had chosen Regina or Winnipeg, we would have loved it the same way.

Our families in Southampton understood my parents' decision. They were sad we were leaving, but now that travel was easier to access, we would see them again. My father's boss was more upset. He tried to convince my father to stay because he really liked how my father put care and pride into his work. He also tried to pay him more, but since it was a union shop, he could only offer a small raise. My father had a lot of respect and appreciation for his boss, and felt bad about leaving, but he had secured this new path and needed to take it.

On May 1, 1966, having sold our house in England to a family member and distributed our belongings, we arrived in Canada with just our suitcases and our dreams for a new life. It was a bright and sunny day, just like the photos in the High Commission. Stepping out of the airport, my father said that everything looked so clean and big. The roads were on a scale he had never seen.

My parents had given me the name Ajit at birth, which means "unconquerable" and "a winner." I would say it was a fitting name, given the challenges I would encounter. At the age of two, they started calling me Sam for no reason except that they liked the name. Sam gradually became my preferred name. So it was as Sam that I arrived in Vancouver on an Air Canada jet when I was about four years old. I don't recall much about the flight, but Air Canada has been our go-to airline ever since.

Back then, for any immigrant accepted on the trades qualification, the government gave the family a travel voucher that could be paid back with no interest and over a long period of time. As a family, we never enjoyed holding debt, so we paid it off as soon as possible. We landed on a Sunday, and through Manpower my father got a job on Monday and started working on Tuesday, at North Shore Sash and Door. Back then, that is how quickly things could work out for a family with the right qualifications.

My arrival in Canada was not easy for me because it happened against a background of lies and deceit. My parents had told me that my beloved tricycle, which I had used to go up and down Derby Road, would be in Vancouver when I got there, and it was not. Years later, I saw photos of my cousins in Southampton riding it. I was not impressed.

Life was nothing out of the ordinary, as I went to school, made friends, and played a lot. It was a simple time and a simple life. England and Fiji were distant for me; I had no physical connection to Fiji, and with every passing day, my roots in England were becoming faint memories. I adapted well to my Canadian lifestyle, slowly becoming more Canadian (whatever that might be) and less Indian. Part of it was a matter of pushing my Indian origins away, as I did not want to be seen as different. My Hindi was limited before I moved to Canada, and once here, I began to lose more and more.

Fortunately, my mother would not allow us to forget our Indian roots with her cooking and her occasional religious services that reminded us of our Indian heritage. She was the connection to a part of the world that was not too familiar to me. We did not have a lot of family in Vancouver at the time, so my Canadian friends through primary and secondary school became my connection to the larger culture and society. Even television at the time was limited—we had a black-and-white unit at the outset and maybe three or four channels.

So we began our life in North Vancouver and settled in. I went to school with my brother, my father continued to work, and my mother got a job at Woolco. As with any family, a routine quickly established itself, and eventually we sponsored families from England and Fiji to join us. We corresponded with relatives in England as that family had grown as well. We saw a shift and exodus of family from Fiji to Canada, England, and the United States.

4

MY
WORLD
SHIFTS

FEBRUARY 10, 1972, is a day I will always remember and the marker that eventually led me to India to find my ancestral roots. That day sealed our family's fate and changed everything in an instant.

I came home from school like any other day. As I entered the house, my aunt was there and she made a cup of tea and told me, before I went out again to play with my friends, that my father had had an accident. The vision in my mind was of my father's car rolling into a ditch and him getting out and walking home. However, that is not what happened. He was at work and they were moving machinery. The cables broke on the freight elevator and it slammed to the ground from three floors up, with heavy machinery and my father inside. There were two other fellows inside as well, and all were hurt. The impact was so devastating that it shattered his legs and jammed his spine. He became a paraplegic, and never walked again.

The vision of the car accident that I held and still hold is not what happened, but it is the image that I know. I am not sure why the elevator mishap does not resonate with me. What is a vivid memory, though, is the shocked and pale look of my mother when I saw her later that evening. She was at a loss for words, and tried her best to maintain her composure in front of my brother and me.

A couple of days later, I was allowed to see my father in the hospital. I was told that they were unsure about the extent of his injuries, but they did know that his spinal column was severed and he was going to be a paraplegic. A paraplegic? When you're nine and a half years old, it is hard enough to say "paraplegia," let alone know what it is. All I understood was that he would never walk again. In the hospital, he was strapped into something called a Foster bed. It was as though he was in a sandwich, with two thin mattresses and straps holding him in place. Every couple of hours, staff would come in and flip him over so that he was not in one position for a long time. They were not sure of the extent of the spinal injury, so they kept him very stable. When he was in the down position, facing the floor, I remember having to crawl under the bed so I could look up and see his face.

There was a long recovery period at G.F. Strong Rehabilitation Centre. G.F. Strong worked to make my father independent. We visited him every day, and as young boys it was a novelty for us, as we would wait for the food tray to arrive to see what we could consume. The nurses on occasion would slide my brother and me an extra tray or treat, which we attacked and devoured. We also attended social activities, such as bingo, and made friends with some of the recovering residents. We were adopted by many of them as companions, and they were always pleased to see us and would ask my father every day if we would be coming in.

After he was discharged, he eventually got back to driving, by using hand controls in his car, and that was always cool to see. We also had an elevator installed in our house, and my friends would come over because it was such a novel thing and we would take them for rides. G.F. Strong taught him to cook and he made himself a modest array of meals. I would come home from school at lunchtime to check on my father and have a bite. One day it was grilled cheese and tomato sandwiches, the next day it was tomato with cheese grilled, and the next day it was toast with cheese and tomatoes. To this day, I don't like cheese and tomato sandwiches or any combination of the sort, but this was the extent of my father's culinary skills.

This incident obviously altered our family's direction. My mother kept working, we went to school, and my father looked after the house. A life lesson that I learned at a very young age is that time is precious. From about ten years old, I realized that life holds no guarantees and that all of us walk a fine line that we sometimes forget.

This is the reason I don't waste my time on negative situations or people. As a family, we don't dwell on the negative aspects of February 10, 1972, but rather see it as a situation we had to deal with. We could have viewed it as a totally negative development and spiralled out of control. Instead, we took a breath and said, "Okay, this is the hand we have just been dealt and we have to work with what is provided."

Some might say that my childhood was robbed from me because I had to take on greater responsibilities and grow up pretty fast. Actually, I had a normal and enjoyable childhood, with some differences. I went out with friends and played games, but I always had one eye on what was going on at home, making sure that all was fine. My childhood was intact.

But my brother and I did have a lot of responsibilities thrust upon us at a young age. My world became concentrated at home after my father's industrial accident, as I felt I had a duty to help the family. I did not venture overseas until I was sixteen years old, and that was to visit England again.

As time passed, more family members immigrated to Canada, many of them to Vancouver. I was reunited with cousins, aunts, and uncles, but I still didn't feel a real need to reconnect to my Indian roots. I would participate in some Indian celebrations, but I did not know what they were about. We all spoke English, and while our parents might speak to us in Hindi and we could understand it, our responses were always in English. My only real connection to England now was letters that my paternal grandmother and I exchanged over the years, but all of those were in English, too. She wrote the odd one in Hindi for my parents, and while the writing looked interesting, it made no sense to me.

When I was thirteen, my maternal grandmother moved from Fiji to Canada. She was more traditional and spoke very little English. I spoke very little Hindi, so how to communicate? Through association, I started to rekindle some words and began to string them together in rudimentary fashion. I had no fluency, but at least we could communicate. This also meant that as Indian religious holidays came about, I got to understand them a little better. However, they still made little sense to me. I did not know the difference between Sikh, Hindu, and Muslim as we never really went to any temples or mosques except for weddings. As a young teenager, those were boring events, and eventually my brother and I opted to stay home rather than partake in such ceremonies. My parents never really bridged the cultures, not because they did not want us to know but more because they were focused on our life in Canada.

Primary and secondary school were fairly uneventful. I was awkward and shy. I did not get into trouble, just quietly blended into the student population. I was not one of the popular kids, not an athlete, not involved in extracurricular activities. I struggled in a few classes, did well in others. My name, Ajit, was in my official school records, but I was embarrassed by it during my childhood and early teen years. I always felt a need to rush in before the first class of the year and inform the teacher before attendance was taken that there was an error and that, while my name might be listed as Ajit, it was actually Sam. I felt that if "Ajit" was called out, I would be singled out as different. I worried that people might say, "Ajit, what kind of name is that?" Ignorance and shame prevented me from embracing my name and blocked me from moving forward. Until I accepted my name, it was a challenge to blend in my Indian heritage.

In elementary school, I always saw myself as Canadian because everything about me reflected the Canadian lifestyle. This changed in high school. With only a small handful of Indian and Asian kids, the vast majority were white Canadians. I recall in grade eight walking along the hallway and being thumped very hard by a much bigger kid for no reason except that he did not like Indians. But wait, I was Canadian, did he not know that? Unfortunately, he saw a skinny brown kid who was different. I got a thumping whenever he saw me in the hallways, and I tried to avoid him at all costs. At times, it was a game of cat and mouse. A couple of other students also felt a need to pick on me, but fortunately it was not that often, maybe because I was unassuming and always stayed in the background.

No matter how hard I tried to fit in, I was always Indian to some and Canadian to myself. I think it was for this reason that I never really enjoyed high school. I couldn't fit in. I went through the motions of going to classes but never really got involved. It is a part of my life that I like to think ignited bigger things that would happen later.

Ganesh is the god of overcoming obstacles, and on February 10, 1972, our world shifted forever. This one was an obstacle that I would never truly overcome.

At home, we would eat Indian dishes or the kind of food my Canadian friends were eating. I wanted to have TV dinners, hot dogs—the same stuff as my friends. On occasion my mom would say that I could take Indian food to school if I wanted. But that was totally out of the question! What if my friends were having sandwiches and all of a sudden I pulled out a roti with curry? I remember one day, when she might have been rushed, she snuck in an Indian lunch of roti and leftover curry. I dumped it in the rubbish bin and bought fries and ketchup in the cafeteria. It was only food, but it was enough to make me draw my line in the sand on what was acceptable or not acceptable.

At Simon Fraser University (SFU), I began to embrace this other side of myself that I'd always tried to hide. I found more of a mix of students and started to connect with my Indian roots. I grew curious about what it meant to be Indian. I found that I went to more functions with Indians, and I learned more about the cultural differences between Hindus, Sikhs, and Muslims, and even about the differences among Hindus. However, I still saw all of us as Indian. My Indian friends shared their food and their cultural upbringing, and it made me start to realize what I was missing. I will always remember my close friends in university, because they accepted me as I was, and we forged long-lasting relationships.

But it was not enough simply to accept my Indian heritage; I was interested in becoming "more Indian." I first noticed this transition in university, because it no longer mattered to me if instructors called me Ajit.

There were students from all around the world at SFU, and I realized that people did not flinch or look about when my name was called. Maybe people did not really care that my name was Ajit. Now that I was trying to catch up to what I had lost, I started to thirst for more knowledge of Sikhism, my ancestral faith, as well as Hinduism. I began learning about the cultural aspects, and I even started to wear a *kara* (a steel bracelet to denote a Sikh).

I had an awakening when my brother and I decided to make our first trip to Fiji with some of our Canadian aunts, uncles, and cousins. We were going to meet family in Fiji for the first time, and I needed to ask my parents who all these people were before we left. This trip was important to me because I wanted to see where my parents and family members were from—the immediate links to our past. I knew very little about Fiji, except as my parents had described it: paradise. I knew there was a native population and an Indian population.

Steve and I left for Fiji with instructions from our parents: be respectful to people you meet, enjoy the fresh fruit, and don't tell anyone you eat beef! We were reminded about my father's interaction with his uncle when they met in England. This instruction took us by surprise, but it was more about how Fijians of the Hindu faith would find it offensive. And some family members did ask us, because we came from a Western society where it was commonly consumed. We responded with a convincing no. Again, this is where I started learning more and more about the cultural aspects of being Indian.

After a long flight, we landed at 1 a.m in Nadi. I recall the plane's door opening and being hit with the night-time heat, humidity, and the smell of sugar cane. There was an entourage of uncles with vehicles to pick us all up, and my brother and I settled with our luggage into the open back space of one uncle's yellow Holden UTE, a hybrid car and pickup truck. As we drove from Nadi to Lautoka, a forty-five-minute journey, we took in the passing scenery and the sugar cane fields. The roads were relatively empty at this time except for the convoy of vehicles coming from the airport. It was dark, so that we could distinguish only the shadows of the mountains around us. We passed small metal shacks with fluorescent tube lights that cast a dull glow, and I could make out men sitting around. As we quickly drove by, we heard blaring Bollywood tunes. The ride was refreshing, and I was eagerly absorbing this new experience.

We got to our relatives' house in Lautoka at about 3 a.m., and our cousins were still up and awaiting our arrival. No one slept, and I remember going out to the veranda and listening to the activity around me: the wind rustling through the coconut trees, the orchestra of croaking frogs and crickets. As dawn approached and the sky began to turn orange, I could make out the silhouette of the palm trees, the doves began to coo, and the roosters in nearby compounds started to crow in unison, awakening the resting community. For the first time, in the distance, I could faintly hear the Muslim call to prayer, penetrating the morning air. It sounded so exotic.

Fiji was fascinating. For the first time in my life, I saw more people like me than in any other place I had been. It was a sea of Indian and native Fijians. It was far easier to find Indian food than Western food. Women were dressed in saris and Indian suits, and this was their everyday wear. I spent time with family members in different places. I tried out my Hindi when I could and found that people would snicker and sometimes laugh, because I tried to do English-to-Hindi translations. It was sneaky on their part, because they would ask me questions and wait for my reply, knowing it would sound different. I started to become very comfortable speaking in Hindi, even if it came out wrong. Walking around in flip-flops, shorts, and T-shirts, I tried to fit in. While many people spoke English, they would throw in Hindi at times. They still saw us as foreigners, but it was not as difficult as I thought it would be.

My brother and I settled in there, and would walk to town or take the bus. We even started watching Bollywood films in the cinemas, but it was very difficult to understand the storyline because there were no subtitles and everyone talked so fast. We were trying to understand why music would suddenly start (where was the band?), the actors would change clothes, and dancing people would show up in fields. It did not make any sense. Watching the movies gave me my first glimpses of Indian culture, and I started to think it might be an interesting place to visit, so I could find those fields of dancing people and music. I actually started to enjoy being Indian and learning about what that meant, and began to better value the difference between Sikhs, Hindus, and Muslims. I appreciated that Fiji is a blend of cultures. My trip there allowed me to dip my toe into understanding Indian culture and being accepted as a foreigner.

My brother and I made a few trips back to Fiji over the years, and we even got our parents to come with us on occasion. They revelled in showing us where they had lived, how to properly eat sugar cane, and where they would go swimming, and they introduced us to even more family. Learning about my parents' history and being able to see life in Fiji ignited a need to learn more, and I think it helped to bridge my Canadian-Indian background. I waded into an understanding rather than being thrown into the deep end.

On one of our trips, my brother got engaged. While my brother and I were close, he started spending a lot of time with his fiancée, leaving me to my own devices. I was introduced to my new sister-in-law's family, and one in particular stood out. She was young and fair-skinned, with captivating hazel eyes. We spent time talking and people could sense that something was up. I was in Fiji for three months, and after I left, we continued to write. One day, my brother's father-in-law asked if we wanted to get married. I wondered, had they been reading our letters?

I married Sadhna while I was in university studying business and political science. The business major was practical, while the political science was out of interest. I was twenty-two and she was just twenty, and she lived in Fiji. Ours was not an arranged marriage, but many people thought we made a great couple. So, in Fiji, on July 14, 1984, we were married in a Hindu ceremony. Here you have someone who is quite unfamiliar with the intricacies of Hinduism and Indian culture going through a complicated ceremony. This was where I really wished there were subtitles, because even though an impromptu interpreter was there, I got caught up in the marriage ceremony and might not have fully understood all the symbolism that was part of the ceremony. I just did what was asked of me. Sadhna moved to Canada six months later, and then I had even more exposure to my Indian background, because she is a devout Hindu. We lived with my parents for a number of years as this was convenient and practical.

Upon graduating from university, I struggled to get my first real job. I did not have an easy go of it as I did not know what type of job or career I was suited for. I applied for many jobs but kept being rejected. In total, I received about eighty-six job rejections in a year. Finally, things improved and I got hired. I wound up being a janitor in a hospital for the first year while I tried to establish myself. That job taught me three valuable life lessons. First, my father always said to do the best job possible no matter what you are doing, so I did, and there was no floor cleaner than at the end of my shift, and no rubbish bin left full. Second, I would get on the elevator at times and the doctors, nurses, and administrators would not acknowledge me because I was a janitor, so I make a point of always speaking to everyone. Third, I realized that I should not deal in absolutes: because I had a degree on my wall but was working as a janitor, people said I was wasting my time. Instead, I decided to use the experience as a chance to learn valuable life lessons.

My next job was at Woolco, while my mother was working for the same business but in a different store. I was in their management program, but that was not a great fit as I had a tyrant boss. I made my first career leap because I did not like being yelled at; I thought only my mother could do that appropriately! So I moved to the Insurance Corporation of BC (ICBC) as an adjuster. They had a position in Smithers, a smallish town of 5,000 in the centre of British Columbia. There were only four Indian families in the town, and they sought us out very quickly. They had known we were arriving before we even got there. I liked the community a lot, and I think the concentration of four Indian families gave me a lot of exposure to Indian culture. One was a Muslim family from Fiji. They were very caring families and they all became part of my extended family, as we would meet every weekend. I learned more and more about my Indian background and, through the Fijian Muslim family, got a grounding on what it meant to be Indian from Fiji. After a sixteen-month stint up north, I moved back to Vancouver and spent many years in claims adjusting and road safety.

I transitioned out of ICBC after thirteen years and started working on the bid to get the 2010 Olympic Winter Games to Vancouver. It was an exciting opportunity and one that created long-lasting friendships. I am still amazed that I got to be a part of one of the most significant projects ever to happen in Vancouver, and I am proud of how we worked so hard and pulled together as a solid team. During the Olympics, I was a spectator and got to see our vision play out. After I finished working on the bid, I decided to take some time off and under-take a journey to India to find my roots.

During this time, in a return to the place where I had studied, I started working at Simon Fraser University, and spent many years engaging and mentoring students in their personal and professional development. I wanted to give students an edge and a solid footing so they would not encounter the rocky start that I had. This then transitioned into teaching and engaging even more students who then went on to become professionals.

BETWEEN APRIL 2003 and November 2004, I started researching my roots. My curiosity had been building over the years, and I wanted to learn more about my background. I sat and listened to my elders talk about their life in Fiji and relate stories about their generation. They also shared historical aspects of their own parents' lives. A realization hit me that their stories, which were handed down orally, had gaps or limited information when they went beyond their own generation. I started to ask them about the village of Chodauri, the post office in Garhshankar to which my father posted letters on behalf of my grandfather, and the district of Hoshiar-pur. I was intrigued by my identity as a Sikh and began to inquire about what that meant.

When I went outside the family to seek information, people chimed in and told me that they knew Hoshiar-pur and Garhshankar, but no one recognized the village name. They said that maybe it was wrong or I was mis-taken. I did not have much to go by, just those three place names. I realized that the research was not going to be straightforward or as easy as finding someone who knew exactly where the village was. Part of the issue was that I was not from India, so all of this was foreign to me.

The more people I asked, the more I came up against dead ends and doubts about finding my grandfather's house. Also, people did not seem to fully understand why I was trying to find my roots. Some thought it was not important to dive into family history, because it did not really matter where you come from. Others said that I might not get a good reception in the village, should we be lucky enough to find it, because it might be thought that I was there to lay claim to the property belonging to my grandfather. And some felt that it was too big a challenge and that maybe I was too immersed in something that was unlikely to materialize. I was astounded to realize that some people are not interested in knowing about their ancestors.

I looked at maps of India and the state of Punjab. Google was helpful for finding the district and post office, but all efforts to locate the village of Chodauri turned up blank. There is a website called mypind. com (*pind* is the Indian term for village) and again I could find the district and post office but no Chodauri. I tried different spellings, such as Chadauri, Chaadauri, Chodori, Chodouri, and so on. Still nothing.

In short, I could not locate the village, people were not overly helpful, and I really did not know the area.

I shared with Sadhna that I felt it was time to visit India to seek out my grandfather's house. I think Sadhna, who also had not been to India, was far more interested in the historic sites and shopping than my crazy plan. She would go along with it as long as the quest did not consume the entire trip. We sat down and started to plan out the trip and how we would get around. Week one would be orientation, week two would be the journey to find the village, and week three was left open for anything we decided we wanted to do; we might need more time to find the village, so we gave ourselves some flexibility. We decided to concentrate on a few areas rather than try to cram the whole country into three weeks. We knew that India would be a culture shock for us both.

We booked our flights from Vancouver to Toronto, and then from Toronto to Delhi. We also found an agency that could get us a car, driver, and guide. Then came the hotels and trying to navigate the location and reviews. Slowly, we tackled our checklist of necessities. I was obsessing about this trip and looking at various hotels and places to visit. I was becoming more and more excited, but also more nervous.

As I was mentally preparing for this voyage, I reached out to various family members to see if there were any further clues. I asked my cousins in California, my father's older brother Ranjit's daughter and son, if they had any information about the village, any shreds of information to go by. Unfortunately, they said they did not. But two days before we left on our trip, I received a letter from my cousin in California. In the envelope was a faded photograph. Ranjit had taken it on one of his trips to the village. He had passed away, so I couldn't ask him for directions to the village. Here, at least, was one physical piece of the puzzle to go by.

The day before we left for India, I received an e-mail from my step-cousin in Fiji. He had heard I was going on this journey and told me he had made a trip to India and got to Garhshankar but did not find the village. He said that I was mistaken and the village name was Janodi (pronounced Jan-OO-dee). Now I felt some momentum. I had a photograph and a name that could be the village. I shot over to mypind.com and searched Hoshiarpur. There was no Janodi, but there was a Jandoli (Jan-DOO-li), which, if said correctly, could sound a bit like Chodauri or Janodi. Jandoli was eight kilometres from Garhshankar, which is where we understood our village to be. With renewed enthusiasm and confidence, I wrote all this information down in my journal.

The day to leave for India arrived and my backpack was ready, as was Sadhna's large suitcase. I had my journal and a book about India, as well as some zip-lock bags, tucked into the backpack pockets. The journal and book were to help in our exploration of India, and the zip-lock bags were to be used in case I found my village and needed a memento. We were dropped off at the airport and made our way to the gate. I was not sure of what life was like in India. People had tried to prepare me for the journey, with mixed reviews. I was told how noisy and busy it would be, how people would not really understand us and we would be seen as foreigners, and how chaotic India could be when compared with Canada. Amidst all this was another perspective: that India is a country with a rich history, amazing food, and variety of cultural experiences.

I sat in the departure lounge and took out the photo of our village. Who were these people? Were they still alive? Over the PA system came the announcement to board.

5

FEET ON
THE GROUND...
BUT NOT
FEELING
GROUNDED

"**L**ADIES AND GENTLEMEN, we are thirty minutes away from landing and we will be beginning our descent."

Well, they say thirty minutes, but it often feels like the longest leg of the journey. I equate it to the concept of Indian Standard Time (IST). You say thirty minutes, but you mean over an hour. I sat there musing about IST and Indian weddings—how you can be on time if the invitation says 6:30 p.m., but you are likely the only one there, and everything starts about 8 p.m. if you are lucky.

After twenty-four hours of being in the air or at airports, the last thirty minutes became the most challenging because I just wanted to get off the airplane. The seat had become more uncomfortable, my ears were

It felt as though I was behind a façade. While I could see out,
I could only see segments—I had to add my own interpretations
of what it meant it be Indian.

raw from the headphones, and my neck was sore from my head bobbing and trying to sleep. The hands on my watch seemed to have stopped moving.

I nudged my wife from her restful sleep and informed her that there were only thirty minutes until landing. "Oh, we are almost there," she said. "That was not that bad." I stared at her in disbelief.

Only darkness below, no horizon or lights. Being surrounded by darkness was making me anxious. A few more minutes passed with still no sign of life, only blackness and a moon to guide us. The calmness seemed to break as the lights from the plane bounced off the clouds below us. We bobbed up and down a bit, swayed with a slight nudge as we caught air pockets.

Finally, with a last heave, the plane broke through the clouds and there before me were the dotted lights of New Delhi, glimmering like mini candles. It reminded me of Diwali, the Indian celebration of lights, where Hindus light many earthen candles that, combined, create a warm glow to break the darkness. It's strange how from a plane at night, every city seems to look the same.

Finally, the lights got larger and closer. I held on to the armrest a bit tighter, and with a sudden jolt we touched down. It was a bit of a hard hit, but a safe landing nonetheless.

With reverse thrusters on, we started slowing down. "Ladies and gentlemen, welcome to New Delhi, where the local time is 11:55 p.m."

With a slow crawl, we taxied to the gate. As we were rolling along, I could hear distinct clicks as a few passengers got ready to dash for the door. We stopped and some people got up, and the flight attendants had to shout at them to sit down again as we were not at the gate. I think the pilots were stopping and going just to have the passengers stand up and sit down. Finally, the plane came to a stop. There was a *bing* and the seat belt sign was no longer illuminated, and in a chorus of clicks we finally undid our seat belts and stood again. The line started moving and we inched closer to the door. Every so often, someone tried to sneak past us to get out more quickly. As the door opened, I was embraced by a blanket of humidity. It was after midnight, but I could feel the heaviness of the air.

I marched with Sadhna to immigration and customs. At first it felt as if I was in a typical airport, but there was also an air of difference: lots of marble flooring and walls, as well as people pressing their hands together and saying "Namaste" with a smile.

We quickly dropped into a mass of travellers, converging and mixing together like blood flowing through veins. The massive immigration area had a sea of people and lines that looked somewhat organized. We made our way to the foreign passport holders' line.

As we waited, I glanced around and saw a beautiful array of colour—women in saris and suits that looked like the plumage of a peacock, with no two outfits the same, and men in traditional outfits called kurta pyjamas, which are long cotton tunics with matching trousers. I was flooded by noise. Everyone was talking and there were many languages being spoken. While looking around, I was bumped by a man likely in his fifties. He turned around, put his hands together, smiled, and with a side-to-side nod said, "Very sorry, sir." I smiled back and put my hands together and acknowledged that it was no problem.

Slowly, step by step, we made it to the front of the line. I handed our passports to two immigration officers. A few quick page flips and then a *stamp, stamp*, page flip, *stamp*. It all looked mechanical. The officers handed us our passports without a glance and waved us to the left. We were now free to enter India.

We found our baggage carousel and the wait began. It was now 12:45 a.m. Luggage snaked past us and was gradually collected until there was only a handful of people remaining. We all recognized each other from the Vancouver–Toronto flight.

An attendant came up to us and told us that our luggage was in Toronto. With a convincing smile and head bob, as if she had solved all our problems, the attendant said, "We will get your luggage here in the most quickest and fastest way possible, sir."

"Okay," I said, "so what is quick and fast?" Deep inside, I knew what the answer would be.

"It will be here on the next flight, so tomorrow, sir, and we will ship it directly to your hotel." And she smiled and bobbed her head again, as if all was totally fine and solved.

No change of clothes, no personal items, and no toiletries for twenty-four hours, just the clothes we were wearing and the small backpack we were carrying. I usually carried an extra pair of clothes, but of course the one time I did not do this, my luggage did not arrive.

We filled out some paperwork, received a verbal confirmation that there would be a small allowance permitted, and were told to keep the receipts, and finally we were on our way.

While all of this was transpiring, there was a thought in the back of my mind. Was losing the luggage an omen for the rest of the trip? Would I not be able to find the village either?

Disappointed, we walked towards the exit. People rushed past to their waiting families. As the exit door slid open and closed, I caught a glimpse of what lay before us, and it got louder and more daunting with every step. Nervousness began to grip me.

6

THE DOORS
OPEN TO
A NEW WORLD

New Delhi

THE EXIT DOORS slid open and we were facing hundreds of people. We stopped for a moment on the threshold of what felt like order, staring into the abyss of disorder. There was thunderous activity, a sea of people moving around, everyone holding signs and trying to gain attention, calling to us and asking if we needed a ride. As we took our first steps into India, the sliding door closed behind us, *whoosh*. Everything that we held within our control was behind that door. I grabbed Sadhna's hand for reassurance and we slowly walked forward.

Before leaving Vancouver, we had booked a car, driver, and guide for the first week. We would be touring Delhi, Agra, and Jaipur. We had no idea who our guide was, but the agency had told us to exit through the arrivals door and they would be there waiting with a sign. We had been tied up waiting for our luggage for about an hour and a half—would they still be waiting? Our official tour was set to start in less than ten hours and we still needed to get to our hotel to settle in.

I now know how Moses might have felt when he parted the Red Sea. There were people to the left of us and people to the right of us. A metal barrier separated everyone from us as we cautiously walked down the aisles. Individuals seemed to glide in and out with careful precision. We stopped and looked around. I told my wife to look to the left while I searched to the right. We took a few more steps and saw the anxiousness in the eyes of those who thought we might need a ride and who might have the good fortune to gain two foreigners. We took a few more steps and there was still no sign of our guide or our sign. We started to think that perhaps we had come to this place ill-prepared. The humidity was making us feel hot and sweaty. We gingerly took more steps forward.

To the side, a hand waved frantically. He was behind three or four rows of people, but I could just see the sign: *Welcome Mr. and Mrs. Tiara*. The spelling was off, but I didn't care at this point. We caught each other's eyes and I waved back. I saw an excited smile and it seemed that everyone around dropped off. We quickened our pace and made our way to the end of the line.

We were greeted warmly by our guide. Hands drawn together, with a slight head bow, he said, "Namaste." A sense of "we have arrived" hit me and all the incidents of the past twenty-four hours seemed to melt away. He smiled and nodded appreciatively, and pointed to his name tag. He proudly announced, "I am Sanjay and I will be your guide for the first leg of your journey." He said that he had been worried we had missed our flight but he was going to stay until he was sure. "I am your guide, sir and madam, I am here to look after you. You can count on me, sir."

I said, "I sure can count on you, and I am so happy to see you."

Sanjay appeared to be in his late twenties or early thirties. He stood about five foot six and was neither lean nor overweight. Clean-shaven and neatly dressed in a cream kurta pyjama and blue cotton vest, he wiped his forehead with a handkerchief. "Sir, I hope the temperature is fine."

I glanced at him and said, "Just a bit hot, but I will be fine." He smiled approvingly and let me know that the car was air-conditioned.

With that, he looked around. "Sir, you have arrived in India. No luggage, sir?" I had to explain that it was delayed. "No problem, sir. Since you are delayed, we will not do a 9 a.m. start. You check in to your hotel and I will be by at 10 a.m. Is that all right, sir?"

I gave an approving nod and said it was fine. We made our way to our car and driver.

I felt a greater humidity, and the thick stickiness clung to me. The air was heavy with the smell of smoke. I thought, *If this is how it is at 2:30 a.m., what is it going*

When we arrived in Delhi, the old and the new were colliding for me.

TOP   Qutab Minar.

BOTTOM   Lotus Temple, both in Delhi.

to be like during the day? Cars darted in and around each other as we carefully crossed the road, protected by our guide. Our driver saw us from a distance and, with an approving smile and wave, called us over to his white Ambassador car. As we approached, he said in the most confident way, "My name is Narendra Sharma." Narendra's dark skin tone was contrasted by his very cleanly pressed white shirt and trousers, as he dressed in a more Western style than Sanjay. His white clothing made his jet-black hair and moustache stand out. With him standing there next to his Ambassador, the scene had a nostalgic aura, like a black-and-white photo. He was not too tall and a bit roundish, like Sanjay. He gave us an approving smile, drew his hands together, bowed, and said, "Namaste." We reciprocated.

I thought how elegant it is to put your hands together and bow your head and utter, "Namaste," a polite and respectful gesture that unites you with another person. "Namaste" allows us to join together for a moment of appreciation. I thought about another word in Hindi that is as powerful as "Namaste": *pyaar*. *Pyaar* means love, and there are many forms of *pyaar*. The *pyaar* that I am speaking of refers to the appreciation that one has, and it comes from a genuine and authentic place of trying to please someone because you care for them. With multiple variations, it comes down to the basic human need to feel loved and a sense of belonging. We all have moments of *pyaar*. *Pyaar* is as simple as a smile or a random conversation with someone you have never met. It could also be you seeing something and purchasing it, not for yourself but for someone who will really appreciate it. I think the world needs more *pyaar*.

Thoughts of Namaste and *pyaar* faded away as our driver stood there holding the trunk open and looking around for our luggage. Our guide informed him that our luggage would come on the next flight, and his expression said, "I am sorry to hear that." Turned out, he was Hindu, but was from another part of India and spoke a different dialect. A smile is universal, so we just nodded. The driver and guide opened the doors for us. There were two cool bottles of water. I opened one and gulped it with pleasure. Instinctively, I went to grab my seat belt. I had the shoulder strap but nothing to clip it into. Okay, it looked like we were going to have to go without, and this took me back to the days when seat belt safety was not a law in Canada but more of a suggestion. I had survived there, so I was sure I would survive here... or so I thought as I looked around.

The air conditioning started blasting and mixed with Bollywood tunes. We lurched forward, pulling out into the artery of traffic. We began to weave in and out, like everyone else. I saw that the cars, including ours, had their mirrors folded in and that it was like stock car racing. The cars got close enough to touch, but some invisible force field prevented them from doing so. In Delhi, trucks can only be on the roads in the very early morning. Large trucks wove in and out, with small scooters dotted between them. The horns, even at this hour, created a constant symphony. Yellow street lights mixed with a thick layer of smoke to create a haze. I could see cars and small stalls by the side of the road where customers were getting late night/early morning meals or snacks.

I tried once more to casually look for my seat belt. Nope, we were freewheeling, and I held on for safety. I glanced at Sadhna, and she had one hand on the seat in front of her and the other on the seat beside her. I wasn't sure how safe it was to put your arm out in front of you when barrelling down the road in an Ambassador, but what can you do.

Our guide turned around and shared his plans. He was apologetic about the 10 a.m. start but informed us there was much to see, and we could stop to do some shopping, so at least we would have some clothes while we waited for our luggage. We gave an agreeing nod and Sadhna grinned mischievously. She got to go shopping on our very first day!

7

FIRST NIGHT...
OR WAS
THAT DAY?

*The Ambassador
Hotel, New Delhi*

WE FINALLY PULLED in to a long, winding driveway at 3:30 a.m. Exhausted and hungry, we caught our first glimpse of a white building, perhaps four storeys tall. This would be our sanctuary for two nights. As our car pulled up to the hotel entrance, a gentleman in a white tunic and bright-red turban with a matching red sash opened the door. His dress was in the traditional style of Rajasthan, and he stood tall. To complete the look, he had a nicely formed waxed moustache. He bowed and said, "Namaste and welcome to the Ambassador Hotel." He waved us towards the door with his white-gloved hands while another doorman held it open for us.

In the lobby, a young lady dressed in an elegant blue-and-red sari put her hands together and welcomed us.

The cloth of her sari was neatly pleated and a long piece of material was draped over her left shoulder. The blues and reds shimmered under the lights. Her lovely brown skin tone was accented by the red dot on her forehead. Her eyes were dark and she wore a nose stud that glistened under the lobby lights. The staff sprang into action and started looking after us. We sipped lemon water as we registered and handed them our passports. The tightness of my body eased. Though my clothes still felt sticky, the air-conditioned lobby was a welcome relief. I thought, *I need a shower and I need it now.*

Our guide followed us into the lobby and stood to the side and at attention. I got a sense that excellent service was a critical part of our guide's and hotel staff's mandates. As our key was handed over, our guide stepped forward and reminded us that he would be back in the lobby for 10 a.m. I was sure he meant Western time and not Indian Standard Time.

We were guided to the fourth floor and our room. The room was massive, with dark hardwood floors. We realized that we had been given a suite, with a couch, armchair, television, and desk. Maybe the staff felt sorry because we'd arrived without luggage and wanted to make our stay more enjoyable. The coffee table displayed a welcome platter of apples, oranges, and bananas. I realized how hungry I was. In the closet were two fluffy white robes. We might not have our luggage and a change of clothes, but at least we had the robes.

My eyes were burning and felt raw. Could it be from woodsmoke, was there smog, or was I just tired? I placed a damp washcloth over my eyes and got some relief. I ate some fruit as Sadhna took a shower. While seated, I must have fallen asleep, because I was jolted by Sadhna saying that she was done. The shower provided such a tremendous relief, relaxing and comforting. I swayed back and forth as the water poured over me, washing away all the sweat, grime, and anxiety. As I dried myself, I felt revived. I washed my underwear, socks, and T-shirt in the sink, thinking that next time I must pack an extra set of undergarments. I tried to dry them a bit with the hair dryer because I would have to wear them again in a few hours, and then left them hanging on the towel racks and watched as a small pool of water started to accumulate. I was calculating how much time I was going to need for the drying process.

With just the gown on, I slipped between the covers. Sadhna was already fast asleep. I closed my eyes, sighed, took a deep breath, and thought, *We have arrived*. What would the day hold? I tossed and turned. Was it jet lag? The thought of our bags arriving? The anticipation of trying to find my village? Would I enjoy this trip?

I got up and quietly made my way to the bathroom to check on the drying clothes, which were now more damp than wet. I had a bit of concern then, but I figured I would wait a few hours. I grabbed my book on India, settled in on the couch, and unfolded the map. How would I find the village in this huge country? In the distance, I could hear the faint sound of traffic. I pulled out the itinerary and got lost in the book as I focused on the history, culture, and sights. My eyes grew heavy and I leaned back on the sofa . . .

I was awoken by the alarm: 7:30 a.m. I pushed aside the blackout curtains and saw the streets of New Delhi before me. Cars streamed past, and waltzing between them were yellow-and-black three-wheeled scooters, motorcycles, and bicycles. The window was dusty with the Delhi air. I swung the balcony doors open and looked out to the grounds. There were large trees in the court-yard that lined the driveway and tropical plants that made up the grounds. I could smell smoke and thought something was burning nearby. The sun seemed to be trapped behind a haze, giving the scene an orange tinge, and I was not sure if that was smog or just an effect of the sunrise. I stood there for a few minutes and decided it was time to make a cup of tea and see what I could do about our clothes.

Yup, I needed to iron the undergarments as they were not quite dry enough to wear. While I ironed, Sadhna used the hair dryer in our roughly fashioned mini-laun-dromat. We felt fresher, but our luggage dilemma was hanging over our heads. We would check out of our hotel the next morning and then the luggage would be one step behind us.

We made our way down to the hotel restaurant, Yel-low Brick Road, for breakfast. It was a quaint little place with a bit of Indian and North American fusion. We were greeted by a lovely young lady who welcomed us with her hands together. She was dressed in an orange saf-fron sari with a red border. Her hair was neatly pulled back and tied in a bun. Her name was Manu and she gave us a warm and comforting smile.

Our hotel greeted us with a *mala* (lei) of beautiful marigolds.

Sadhna went for the traditional items such as idly (rice flour steamed flying saucers with coconut chutney) and parathas (a bread) with a potato curry. I went for a mix of cultures and got some of the curry and paratha but also added eggs, baked beans, and bacon. I used the bacon to try to keep the items separate because it seemed that by mixing them together, I would be mixing the cultures. I guess my breakfast was representative of my identity, and how I felt divided by being both Indian and Canadian. I glanced at Sadhna's plate and it was a culinary journey through the Indian subcontinent: curries that were rich and heavy from the northern region, and the spicy and watery gravies of the South. I think I preferred her plate, with interesting foods that the locals would eat.

We ordered tea and settled in. The food was far more flavourful than anything I have ever experienced. It was as if someone had stripped away the MSG and replaced it with natural ingredients. Every bite was a unique symphony of flavours. Whether potato, beans, or eggplant, they were all infused with spices that were distinct but not overpowering. Even the level of spiciness was perfect: flavourful but not too intense, with chilies and pickles to the side for the more daring, like Sadhna. I pushed down my fear of getting Delhi Belly or far worse and sat back to enjoy this meal. My second helping was far more representative of the Indian subcontinent.

At 10 a.m., we made our way to the lobby, and there, standing at attention and ready to go, was our guide Sanjay, who was obviously not running on Indian Standard Time! With a wave and smile, he rushed towards us. "I hope you are rested and feeling better this morning." I nodded, though I still felt my slightly damp undergarments.

We stepped out of the safety and comfort of the hotel onto the driveway. There, an Ambassador car rolled forward and we saw our smiling driver, Narendra. The doorman opened our car door and with the flow of his hand and my feet swinging in, we were now on our first day's adventure. I went to grab the seat belt, then remembered there were no seat belts in the car. I braced myself as Narendra began weaving along the driveway to the exit and New Delhi.

8

DIFFICULT LESSON IN BRILLIANCE AND DARKNESS

Jama Masjid

AS WE PULLED UP to the busy street, I saw a constant flow of traffic. Cars, motorcycles, tuk-tuks, hand-drawn carts, rickshaws, scooters . . . If it had wheels or legs, it was on the road. A scooter drove by bearing a family of four—the father driving, a small child standing on the platform near the handlebars, the wife sitting sidesaddle with her infant in her lap. Her green sari waved behind her like a cape as they wove between cars and were gone in a buzzing flurry.

Narendra waited for his opportunity and swung left, and we were in the artery of traffic. Horns were blaring all around us, with no one honking at anyone in particular. People just liked to honk! Narendra had this calm look about him as he manoeuvred in and out of traffic.

He glanced in his rear-view mirror, to his side, to his other side, then repeated the whole thing as if it was mechanical. We slowly passed an emaciated cow in the middle of the intersection, with vehicles going around it. It was not so much sickly as just very thin. I know that the cow is sacred in India and people have a high regard for it, but I wondered how, with so much traffic around, this thin cow had made it to the centre of the intersection. Did it escape, or did it belong there? The cow seemed to not really care about the traffic and just went about its day. I suppose if you are a cow in India, you can do as you wish.

Sanjay turned around and started laying out our game plan. "Okay, since your luggage is not here till later, I will take you to a shop so you can at least get something."

Sadhna's eyes lit up. Clothes! I reminded her that we were doing this out of necessity and not desire, but my words seemed to disappear in the air. "Do they have ladies' Indian suits?" Sadhna asked Sanjay. He nodded, and I felt my wallet already getting lighter.

We arrived at a small shop and were escorted in. There were all shades of fabric and ready-made Indian suits. Sadhna looked around and found a navy blue suit with a beautifully embroidered Kashmiri design. She turned to the storekeeper and he looked at her with a critical eye, reached behind the counter, and pulled out a small stack of similar suits. It seemed as though he had been doing this for many years and had a very good idea about sizes. She tried on the suit and it fit perfectly. She decided she was going to wear it out. With Sanjay, we went back and forth with the shopkeeper and agreed on a price. I knew that we had been taken advantage of, but it was a reasonable price that I was comfortable paying. Living in Canada, I am used to paying the price listed, but I know that in many countries haggling is common practice and required. The challenge is that I think there is a big stamp on my forehead saying TOURIST and that shopkeepers can see me from a great distance and await my arrival.

Back in the car, Narendra started up the Ambassador and, with a jolt, we were on the road again. I braced myself with a hand against the front seat, as if this would help me should an impact occur.

Sanjay told us that we would now start our day of exploring New Delhi. Our first stop would be Jama Masjid in Chandni Chowk. For Muslims, "*masjid*" means a church or place of worship. As we negotiated traffic, I was in awe of the number and pace of people and vehicles. They seemed to be going in every direction, and everything happened quickly. When we arrived at our first destination, an old lady approached our car and tapped on our window. She was wearing a plain and faded sari. Her wrinkles formed pockets on her face, and she was wearing a gold nose ring that glistened in the morning sun. She looked at us and used hand gestures to show she was hungry. Before we could say or do anything, Sanjay, through his open window, told her to leave. She reluctantly walked away, seeming to scowl at Sanjay, but stayed nearby, maybe to ask us again once we got out.

Our first big experience in India was visiting the Jama Masjid in Delhi.

Sanjay turned to speak to us, this time with a bit of a serious tone. We received our first roadside lesson. He told us that you cannot give anything to the beggars because they will crowd around you and you will not be able to get away. Seeing poverty on this large scale was very difficult for us because we could not do anything to intervene. We were inundated with beggars who approached the car while we were still seated within its protective boundaries. We stared straight ahead but could see them in our peripheral vision and could understand what they were saying in Hindi through the windows. "Give us something, please, and we will bless you." "We have nothing, will you not help us?" "I will pray for you if you help us." Sanjay got out of the car and slowly opened the door to let us out. We had about ten people around the car, but they did not touch us. We blindly walked towards the Jama Masjid with Sanjay, and they disappeared into the background.

We were thankful for Sanjay's presence. If we had been here on our own, we were not sure we would have survived. Those who came up to us knew we were foreigners, and foreigners mean money. In India, I was an outsider, a tourist, not a local. However, they spoke to us in Hindi and broken English to cover all the bases and make their plight known. I suppose, in their eyes, we were a different kind of Indian from somewhere far away—a foreigner. To them, it only mattered that we might give them something.

Jama Masjid is the largest mosque in India, built in the mid-1600s. We stood in the massive courtyard and Sanjay told us how it could hold around 25,000 people.

I felt like a speck and could only imagine how crowded it must be when there is a religious function.

We went through a massive entrance and took off our shoes. As we began walking in the open space of the mosque, it was not as crowded or as noisy as the outer areas. Casually strolling about and exploring areas within the walls, I was drawn to the Mughal architecture and art. It is most impressive, and everything is symmetrical and clean. There is an elegance to the scriptures, and while I didn't know what the writings said, they were incredible and I could imagine the poetic beauty locked within the words.

The structure was made of red sandstone and had an earthy and dusty tone. The walls felt gritty under my palm. We walked on the marble floor that was worn out and cool to the touch, smooth like glass and with a solid feel. We approached a set of marble stairs and I stopped to look at them with interest. The stone slabs were indented and worn out in the middle from the continued pressure and presence of people. I know that rivers can alter the shape of stone, and here a river of people had worn out the centre parts of these stones. I liked that they maintained the stones used by pilgrims. Sanjay showed us the different areas and told us the history of the place, and we were out of there in about forty-five minutes.

As we walked back to the car, I saw old women, girls with babies in their arms, a man with deformities sitting on a barrel, and little children all around. There was nothing anyone could do to help because the poverty was so overwhelming. I glanced to the left and saw a man crawling along the sidewalk on all fours like a tired old dog. His head hung down and every movement was in slow motion. His clothes were worn out and ripped in places. A small metal cup scraped the ground with every movement. The hardships that had been dealt to this man were unfathomable. It was as if every single inch forward was a challenge, and people just walked by him as if he did not exist. My mind and heart said stop, but my feet kept moving. I didn't like this feeling one bit.

Looking at these people, I had a sense of their resiliency. They have suffered much, but at the same time, they survive. It is not a good life, but it is a life. I realized that I carry worry as my burden, but I have different worries from the basic needs of these souls. We tend to overcomplicate our lives. I am not saying that they are happy or pleased with where they are in life because external circumstances have dictated their plight, or that we are happy with all that we have. We just put different pressures and demands into our lives. Even though we come from different worlds, we share similar emotions and feelings.

As I sat in the car, my memory of the Jama Masjid paled in comparison with the image of this man crawling along the ground. Humanity has built these magnificent structures that have withstood the test of time, and they provide a refuge to many. But we have such inequality in this world that I wonder which is greater, the structure or the resilience. Yes, there were touristy things to see, but the poverty—as hard as it was to witness—was part of the overall experience.

As our car started to move forward, Sanjay turned and said that the poverty is difficult to explain. Those we saw, for the most part, have a beggar master who feeds them and looks after them, because they are his commodities. "Commodities?" I said. Sanjay explained how any money given to the beggars was collected and lined the pockets of the beggar master, so by giving to the beggars, you are supporting the master. I knew he was trying to put my mind at ease. As we drove away, I balanced the individual suffering around the Jama Masjid with the impressiveness of the structure and how it symbolizes what people are capable of when they put their collective energy together.

I asked myself, how can humanity be so cruel, and how can life deal such a challenging hand to some individuals? On this journey I would see monuments, structures, and temples built with greatness in mind. But intertwined with all this prominence was culture and everyday life, including poverty I could not mask or ignore. I needed to learn acceptance quickly or this trip would become a disastrous experience. I needed to prioritize the search for my village as the most important aspect of the trip. I took a deep breath and closed my eyes. I told myself that this is life, not my life, and that I must not interfere. I felt comfort and safety in the car, but I didn't want the car to be my sanctuary. I wanted to experience this country for all that it was, good and bad. I promised myself that whatever I saw and encountered, I would accept it. I wanted this trip to make me a stronger person. I reminded myself that I'd left Canada behind the doors at the airport and would not make any comparisons, judgments, or assessments. I would accept my experiences as just that—experiences. I would have to accept and embrace anything that was thrown my way, no matter how ill-prepared I was.

I don't think anything prepares you for what you will encounter in India. One can describe life in India, but it is always an understatement. I can only imagine the culture shock someone who is not Indian would experience.

9

ASSUMING SOME NORMALCY

India Gate | Birla House (Gandhi Smriti) | Qutb Minar | Humayun's Tomb

OUR NEXT STOP was India Gate and the parade corridor. We parked on the side of the road. There were lots of people around, but this was nothing like Jama Masjid, and had more of a touristy feel. For a moment it felt like I was in Europe, until I saw a woman dressed in a beautiful blue sari walking by, balancing an earthen water jug on her head. I was impressed by her poise and grace.

India Gate looks like the Arc de Triomphe and was constructed in the 1920s to commemorate all the Indian soldiers who gave their service and lives for their country. It is the centrepiece of an open space where military marches take place. A staggering 70,000 Indians were killed during the Great War, a war that my maternal grandfather survived. I felt that a small part of this monument was dedicated to his service.

We wandered around and I was taken aback by the influence of Indian and British architecture. We could only see the buildings through the huge metal gates. The large space was open and clean, appropriate for the centre and cornerstone of Indian government. I have always been impressed that India has the world's largest democracy, and you sometimes wonder how government functions with so many interests and religions. The country is a kaleidoscope of cultures that always seems to be changing. India seemed so chaotic to me that I wondered how anything could be accomplished.

Sanjay waved us back to the car like a mother calling her children in from playing outside. "We have much ground to cover," he said. Sanjay casually asked if we wanted to visit Birla House, where Mahatma Gandhi was assassinated, or the place where he was cremated. I guess he could have expressed this choice differently: the place where Gandhi lived or the place where his last rites were performed? History has always fascinated me, so we decided to venture to Birla House to see his journey and learn the story behind what happened.

In modern-day New Delhi, "Gandhi Smriti" means "Gandhi remembrance" and is the museum of Mahatma Gandhi. This house is where Gandhi spent the last 144 days of his life. Every morning, Gandhi would walk through the gardens to awaiting pilgrims who wanted his blessing or just to be in his presence. January 30, 1948, was no different. As Gandhi strolled towards the waiting crowd, he was shot four times. It is said that he fell to the ground and uttered his last words, which may have been *"Hai Ram"* or *"Rama Rama,"* meaning "Oh, God!"

We traced his steps from the house to the grounds and to where he fell. His steps are indicated by a reproduction of cement footprints. We were in the presence of greatness and in a place that was very significant in modern Indian history. We sombrely walked around the museum and well-tended grounds. Every so often a horn from a passing car broke the silence, but for the most part it was very quiet.

We spent a lot of time walking the grounds. I was fascinated by all the displays, letters, and objects, as well as the stories embedded in each. I saw the meagre belongings of one of the world's most revered leaders with my own eyes. I saw his bloodstained white robe, and his famous reading glasses.

I think this was the stop I valued most of all that day. I did not feel rushed, and sensed the historical significance of the place. I temporarily stopped worrying about the luggage issue, and embraced the moment. I stood at the small stone monument for what seemed a long time, trying to appreciate what this place held. After what seemed like a decent amount of time, we headed to the exit and our waiting car. Sanjay suggested lunch, and I realized how much time had passed and how hungry I was.

Little did I know that our next stop would be a usual trick and trap. We went to a shop that made carpets. We were given a demonstration and looked at all the intricate work, but the underlying command was: "Buy me!" Our tour guide and the storekeeper were in partnership: Sanjay would bring the customer and hopefully they would purchase a rug. Now, don't get me wrong, these were exquisitely handcrafted rugs and I appreciated the workmanship, but this was only our first day there. I didn't even have a change of underwear, and I should purchase a carpet? We politely declined any rug orders, though I would have gladly purchased clean socks, underwear, and a T-shirt at that point. Sanjay seemed a bit disappointed, but he shrugged his shoulders and I told myself this was probably not the last time we would be seeing a shop of some sort.

After lunch, we headed to the Qutb Minar. This World Heritage Site has been designated as a free-standing minaret and was built in 1193. It is about 240 feet high, with a massive base. It has stood for centuries and has changed meaning over time. It was a Muslim monument, then Hindus claimed they had laid the foundation stones well before, and then the Muslims claimed they had laid stones even before the Hindu ones.

At times, Hindus and Muslims are solid and brotherly with each other; other times, they are as challenging as divorcing partners—back and forth, with no middle ground, and everyone wanting to claim something as theirs. The more I saw, the more I understood that there are layers of influences that span centuries, like sedimentary rocks. I guess that by having moderate parents and an upbringing in another country, I did not really understand the divide. I was always brought up to respect others and not put everyone into categories.

TOP Visiting Humayun's Tomb, offered our first glimpse of brilliance.

BOTTOM Walking the grounds where Gandhi was assassinated, gave me a sense of the history of the fight for India's independence.

The Qutb Minar was a good symbol of India's layered history. Like waves that roll in and recede, Indian history and cultural influences show the presence of Hindu, Muslim, Hindu, Muslim, British, Hindu, Muslim, and so on. After a while the distinctions seem to blend into one another, visible in the architecture, writings, temples, mosques, and people. The arrival of the British made the most impact on the population, introducing a new direction. The younger generation does not seem to embrace as many of the cultural norms as the older people, and this is most evident in their dress. If someone is more orthodox, they will wear symbols and signs, such as the sari or kurta.

I thought about my life and how I create distinct markers of being Canadian, British, Fijian, and Indian. I tended to separate them neatly, but for the first time I started to see a blending, like an artist mixing colours on their palette. I saw shades of my life as a British-born Canadian with Indian and Fijian backgrounds. I realized that the boundaries I had drawn were imaginary, and I started to experience a shift in my sense of who I am. I told myself, *I am Indian!* But that was something that I never really shared or talked about.

As we were walking back to our car, a girl about six years old with straggly hair, an old frock, and no shoes approached us and in broken English asked for some money. She walked at a fast pace and three or four times repeated her request. Finally, my wife turned to her and said in perfect Hindi, "Sorry, we are not able to give you anything." The girl stopped dead in her tracks and looked perplexed, and in Hindi she said, loud enough for us to hear: "That white lady speaks perfect Hindi!" We continued back to the car with smiles on our faces because it was so cute.

Our last stop of the day was Humayun's Tomb. I was actually glad this was the last stop, not just because I was tired but because the place was so impressive. The grounds were beautiful and the architecture was amazing, made of red sandstone and showcasing Mughal ingenuity. Sanjay shared that this was a preview of what was to come, because it is a bit like the Taj Mahal. The grounds were peaceful and I enjoyed walking around undisturbed. I had my camera with me and was looking for all the right angles and shots. I felt excited about seeing this India of glory, magnificence, and mystery. Everything to this point had felt rushed, but here it was all serenity.

I sat on a bench and admired the main tomb area. Mughal emperor Humayun's tomb was there, and the graves of many other noble people. Humayun's Tomb was built around 1570 and was the first garden-tomb in India. I was sheltered by a tree and felt a soft, cool breeze. I wondered, *What was life like back in the day? Who walked in this area? Was it bustling or quiet?* Our architecture in Canada felt so new by comparison. Our First Nations people in Canada created a rich cultural foundation, which incorporated the lives and spirits of animals, trees, mountains, and streams. Their history is deep-rooted, while Canada as a country is relatively new.

I probably sat for about fifteen minutes but then realized that we must head back to our hotel. I needed to follow up with the airlines and sort out the luggage, because the next day we were checking out and on the road to Agra. Also, the long flight was starting to catch up with me. I broke my peaceful silence and walked back to the car feeling somewhat refreshed but tired.

Sanjay seemed content that he had done a good job showing us around. Narendra also appeared satisfied that his driving was appreciated. I was grateful that Narendra was such a skilful driver that we were not hurt or killed.

By the time we got back to the hotel, it was already dark. We made our way up to our room, and we decided to tidy ourselves as best we could before going down for dinner. After, we would go back to the room to shower, change into our robes, and wash our undergarments. All the while I was thinking, *What if our luggage does not arrive on tonight's flight?* We had to check out of our hotel the next day. How would our luggage find us in this confusing and chaotic country? I was wearing my worry again!

I am not sure if I was overtired, if all my senses were overwhelmed, or both, but I could not sleep again. At midnight, I started my calls to the airport to make them aware we needed our luggage. On my first call, the staff said that the flight had not arrived and they would let us know as soon as it did. I sat and waited. At 1 a.m., I made another call, and they advised that the flight had arrived and the bags were being unloaded. I waited for a return call—nothing. At 2:30 a.m., I called again and they said they would try to get it to us as soon as possible.

Finally, at 4 a.m., we got a call from the lobby. Our luggage had arrived! They sent it up, and I grabbed my backpack and embraced it with glee as if it was a long-lost friend. I opened it and snatched up some clean clothes. Wearing a fresh pair of underwear, I grinned and said to myself, *Now my trip can officially begin!*

10

I WANDER
AND SEE
WONDER

Akbar's Tomb |
Agra

EVEN WITH ONLY a few hours' sleep, we were ready to take on the world. I picked out some fresh clothes and we made our way down to breakfast with renewed vigour. Our trip was set up in such a way that we arrived in Delhi, spent a couple of days here, then went off to the Golden Triangle of Delhi–Agra–Jaipur; then we would come back to Delhi for a day and a half and then on to the Punjab to see Amritsar and search for the village. Finally, we would return to Delhi for a short layover. I had planned a loose timeline for our visit to the Punjab and our search for the village. We left our last week somewhat open, though I thought about heading to Jaipur and Udaipur and then concluding our stay in Delhi. Rather than try to see an entire country in three weeks, we concentrated on a section of it so we could really experience the richness of the flavours and experiences. Delhi was going to be our base.

We sought out Narendra and his signature white Ambassador, which is the model of almost all taxis in India and in Bollywood films. He would drive us through Agra and Jaipur, while we would have a new guide for this journey as Sanjay was staying in Delhi. The staff from the hotel stood by the door to say goodbye. They put their hands together in a graceful way, bowed their heads, and said, "Namaste." I had enjoyed my stay so much that I thought we might need to reconsider our future Delhi plans so we could return here.

Narendra wore a wide grin. He too welcomed us by putting his hands together and saying, "Namaste." He was happy to see that we had our bags, pointing to them and bobbing his head from side to side in pleasure. He took the luggage and heaved it into the trunk and opened the doors for us to get inside. We were off on our adventures of the Golden Triangle that sits in the province of Rajasthan. I didn't even reach for my seat belt this time. I felt I must be transitioning into my Indian life.

After a while spent manoeuvring through traffic, we came to an intersection with cars, buses, and everything around us coming to a grinding halt. A massive stream of vehicles were flowing ahead of us, like blood through a major artery. While we waited for the endless stream of traffic to let up, Narendra pointed in one direction and said, "Delhi." Then he traced his finger to the other side and said, "Mumbai." Then, with both hands spread out and a head bob and grin, he said, "Traffic." We were at the crossroads on the main route between Delhi and Mumbai. The traffic seemed endless, but somehow, as though he were skilfully threading a needle, Narendra was able to slip through and then we were on the road to Rajasthan again.

As we stopped for traffic again, I glanced over to the side. I saw a massive heap of garbage running for a couple of city blocks. It was a dumping ground, and children with sticks were going through the piles of trash. Many were barefoot and climbing, poking and looking around. This was their playground. Other children were smiling and playing as if they were searching for hidden treasure. This was their daily adventure and routine, and I wondered if any had ever been outside Delhi.

We drove through the countryside on the road to Agra. The traffic lightened up and we were free to hit the gas and move at a decent pace. Instead of weaving between seven widths of cars on three marked lanes, we seemed now to be gliding along in one lane. The drive was at times quiet and contemplative, and other times we hit pockets of traffic. I caught glimpses of people as we passed. I wondered, *Who are these people? What are their stories, and what are their lives like?* I noticed that there was an abundance of smiles, an image that stayed with me. I will never fully understand and appreciate this aspect of India: no matter how challenging things are, Indians carry on and they do it with dignity. In Canada, children look at toys on television and start to construct their gift-wish lists; in India, children make small wheels out of spool and wire and run around and that brings them joy.

This is how I felt sometimes. Locked out from experiences, I was searching for the key to unlock the door so I could embrace being Indian and not just a foreigner.

After a couple of hours we pulled into a *dhaba* (a roadside café) for some refreshments. We asked Narendra to join us, but he respectfully waved us in. The café was quite empty and dark. We were cautious about what we ate in India because people had warned us about Delhi Belly and how it could ruin our trip. We decided to order chai and pakoras (battered vegetables). I figured pakoras are safe because they have been deep-fried and germs cannot survive an Indian fry-up. The tea was thick, sweet, and freshly made, and the pakoras were crispy and hot. I used the washroom before we got back in the car, and it was really just a hole in the ground with an overwhelming smell. Not a pleasant experience, but I was glad I went after the chai; who knew when our next stop was going to be?

We ordered pakoras for Narendra, which he appreciated, and then we were back on the road. We were in Rajasthan now, and saw women working in the fields, their brightly coloured saris looking like flowers in the distance. It dawned on me that rural Rajasthan is all about richness of colour. We saw reds, pinks, and blues. In many parts of the world, saris are worn for celebrations and religious services, but here they are a way of life. These women work hard in the fields with grace and skill, while wearing yards of beautiful material.

Narendra signalled that we had a stop ahead that was not included in the tour package. I thought this might be another stop-and-shop where he would make a commission. As we pulled up, though, I saw a sign that said *Akbar's Tomb*. In his broken Hindi, he said that we could likely buy tickets at the local rate. It was worth a try. He parked and then walked up to the ticket counter and bought us two tickets with some money we gave him.

He wound up paying only 10 rupees each (in other words, we could get in for 30 cents each rather than $3). I had to make sure not to say a word because our cover would be blown and we would then have to pay the higher price. I would have been fine paying the full price, but Sadhna already had the ticket in hand.

We approached the gate, and the two security officials gave us a quick once-over and looked at our tickets. One guard said in English, "Tourist rate," at which Sadhna explained in fluent Hindi that she was visiting from Delhi and had come out to see this site. They looked at me and said, "What about him?" Sadhna explained that I come from the Punjab but do not speak Hindi. In the one or two Punjabi words I could string together, I tried to fool them. They let Sadhna in for the tourist rate, but I wound up having to pay the full $3. Trying to disguise me as a local is like trying to hide vegetables in a kid's meal—eventually you are found out! So, I was not Indian, still a foreigner? I felt like a butterfly trying ever so hard to break out of its cocoon. I wanted to be accepted and acknowledged as Indian. Maybe I was a different breed of Indian, but still Indian! It dawned on me that I was trying to be Indian in the eye of the beholder but that maybe it was more important whether I felt like an Indian. Maybe if I felt more Indian, others would accept me as such.

We strolled through the grounds, which reminded me of the beautifully manicured gardens of Birla House in Delhi. Walking the path, I could hear the singing birds in the trees that welcomed our arrival. We did not want to disturb the deer grazing on the grass, so we carefully skirted them and approached the structure, which I learned was Akbar's Tomb. From the outside, it looked like a beautiful, symmetrical temple. It had a red-and-pink colour palette. The front was adorned with intricate designs and patterns. The structure blended Islamic, Hindu, Buddhist, Jain, and Christian motifs. Inside, the corridor and the large room were bare—a real contrast to the outside.

Our steps echoed as we neared the main chamber. There was a single marble tomb and nothing else. I don't recall any adornments on the walls or any sort of colour. A single bulb weakly lit the room where the tomb was, casting our shadows onto the walls. As I looked around, I thought that even having other coffins, motifs on the wall, or more light might have made it feel warmer. It seemed very cold and lonely, as if the person who had died no longer had anyone around them. I stood there in silence for a moment, and it was a peaceful quiet that surrounded us. I reflected that maybe this place was representative of how people sometimes feel when they are going through a difficult time: there is an emptiness within, but no one knows about it because the outside looks fine. I left the room and stepped back into the warmth and glow of the sun outside, birds chirping in the distance and deer grazing nearby. I looked up to the sky and the surroundings and appreciated being back in the open air.

We headed back to the car and resumed the drive to Agra. After a couple of hours, the traffic became heavier.

On the outskirts of Agra, Narendra stopped near a residential area and the car door opened. A stout man wearing a white tunic with a waistcoat and a white Nehru-style hat came to greet us. With a very pleasant smile, he introduced himself as Nasser and said he would be our guide for the trip through Agra and Jaipur. As we moved forward, the traffic started clogging up, and before we knew it, we were crawling through Agra. All modes of transportation seemed to be funnelling through a narrow passageway. Nasser asked Sadhna if she had done her shopping yet, as he knew of places we could visit. I was not even included in the conversation.

We parked the car and walked into a Rajasthali tourist shop. Sadhna was amazed by the sari selection. We sat on a bench and the owner sat cross-legged on a stage in front of us and turned on a series of lights. He leaned forward and asked Sadhna what she would like to see, and with a wave of his hand he indicated a wall laden with different materials and colours. Like a kid in a candy store, Sadhna started pointing here and there. They pulled out six yards of fabric in different colours and unfurled it in front of her. Another gentleman next to him stood and draped it on himself. We savoured two cups of steaming hot chai while we were shown the fabrics and Sadhna made her selections. She decided on two saris and two Indian suits. We also purchased a sari for Narendra's wife. We negotiated, knowing full well we were being taken advantage of, but it was within our payment pain threshold. I carried the bags out to the car. When we gave Narendra the sari and explained it was for his wife, his eyes widened with pleasure.

I walked into a neighbouring store and they had men's Indian tunics. Maybe dressing like a local would allow me to feel more like one. I tried one on and the sleeves were three-quarters in length. The salesman said with a head bob, "Sir, that is fashion . . . three-quarter sleeve." Suspicious, I tried on the pants that went with it, and they too came out to three-quarter length—mid-shin. He looked at me and I said, "Ummm, you are not going to say this is fashion, are you?" He grinned and let me off the hook by replying, "Sir, that is not going to fit you." In India, they will try to sell you everything and anything by painting a rosy picture, but it wasn't working in this case! I looked around and settled upon a burgundy linen long tunic that went to my mid-thigh.

We arrived at an open-air lot and Nasser hopped out and opened our door. He explained that our luggage would be safe in the vehicle and that we were going to switch into one of these low-emission vehicles because they were trying to clean the air around the Taj Mahal. We got into a golf cart and headed towards our destination. At a park, we pulled over and got out. The park was peaceful, with only a few people and vehicles around us. Nasser walked up to the gates and handed our tickets to two uniformed guards. Then we stepped into one of the most magnificent sites I have ever experienced.

11

EXTRAORDINARY
IN THE
ORDINARY

Taj Mahal

W E TOOK a few steps forward through an archway, and there before us stood the Taj Mahal. I was in awe, just taking it in. It stood prominently, a brilliant white marble structure with four minarets rising on the corners. From a distance, it looked like an ornament—something to be admired but not touched. People were walking by me, but I did not pay attention to them and just stared. It was about 3 p.m. I was told that the pure-white marble would change colour throughout the day based on the sun. I glanced up and saw that the sun was a large orange ball, and realized what Nasser meant: the smog was quite thick and it was giving everything a reddish tint, but the Taj Mahal's white brilliance had only a hint of slight orange.

We walked down the stairs, around the grounds, past guides and photographers, and saw that there were two accompanying structures on opposite sides, with the Taj Mahal in the centre. Everything was balanced and neatly arranged. Nasser continued to point out interesting facts here and there, but I was not really paying attention as I was captivated by the beauty of the Taj Mahal and it was drawing me in. As we walked alongside the fountain and got closer to the main building, I could really admire the intricate work. We walked up the stairs and stood outside the entrance. The marble was so bright that I had to squint and could not see a thing due to the glare of the sun on the brilliant white walls. I took my shoes off and stood on the cool, slick marble floor. I touched the walls of marble and it was nothing like the gritty sandstone of the Jama Masjid. Instead, it was smooth, soft, and silky.

We walked inside and I saw that the white marble walls were adorned with complex patterns and designs of varying colours. Some were intricate lattice designs that made me wonder about the workmanship and tools they used, because carving machines were not available then and even if they had been, they could likely not produce the quality of work these people had achieved. The floor was also patterned in black-and-white marble like a massive chessboard. The designs looked flawless. With a flashlight, Nasser explained how craftsmen created these walls and that you can always tell authentic craftsmanship from fake knock-off marbles that vendors might try to sell you. He showed that if the light passes through the marble, it is not designed like the Taj

Mahal. He took a piece of patterned marble that looked like a part of the wall and put his flashlight to it, and sure enough, the light just went through it, appearing dully on the other side. But when he held his light up to the wall of white marble, the intricate colours came to light and seemed to glow like a kaleidoscope, dancing in a sea of brilliance and colour.

Walking along the corridors, I was struck by the building's magnificence. Any pictures I had seen did not do this place justice. We came to the centre of the complex, which was lit by natural light. Again, everything seemed symmetrical, with one exception: right in the centre of the complex was the large stone tomb of Mumtaz Mahal, the wife of Shah Jahan. He was a Mughal emperor and he built this tomb for his wife when she passed away. Their tombs are next to each other and are similar but also a little different—his a bit larger than hers, and offset from the centre.

He built the white Taj Mahal structure for the wife he had loved so much. His dream was to build another Taj Mahal in black, across the Yamuna River from her, for himself. But due to a feud with his sons, he was imprisoned and died in the Agra Fort. Since his black Taj Mahal dream was never realized, his sons put his coffin next to hers. The room was not symmetrical, but at least he was beside her. The tomb room was appropriately quiet, and it seemed out of respect that one would not speak here.

Nasser signalled to us and we followed him outside. He said that we could look around on our own for a while and took his leave. I took out my camera to capture the Taj Mahal at various angles. We were randomly pestered by guides who wanted to explain the structure and trivial facts. Photographers also bothered us, offering to snap our photo for a small fee. These disruptions prevented me from really appreciating the outside, much like when someone is whispering a conversation right behind you in a movie theatre.

Sadhna and I found that on one side of the grounds was a mosque and on the other side was a fake mosque. It made total sense, because a true mosque is designed to face Mecca, but the other one would not. The fake mosque was there to keep the grounds symmetrical. I knew that we had time the next morning to visit the grounds again, but just in case the timing did not work out, I wanted to absorb as much of this place as possible.

We walked to the waiting cart, where we met Nasser, and together we travelled to the car. I felt satisfied, as though I could now tick off one of the main reasons I had come to India. Two more to go: the Golden Temple of Amritsar and my village. Did I feel more of a connection to India after seeing the Taj Mahal? No. Rather, wearing my tourist hat allowed me to appreciate its beauty.

It was now about 5 p.m., and we were tired and getting hungry. Narendra started towards our hotel and I noticed how crowded and dirty Agra was. The streets were narrow, people were everywhere, and things seemed disorganized. I started getting agitated, but for Narendra, this was life. Finally, we arrived at our hotel. It was a nice-looking building, and we were happy to finally be able to relax and grab something to eat. Nasser let us know that they would pick us up the next morning.

Seeing the Taj Mahal was one of the highlights of our trip—it did not disappoint!

We checked in and made our way to the room, where I crashed on the bed to stretch and relax.

Shortly afterwards, Sadhna said to me: "I am going to tell you something, but you have to promise that you are okay with what I am going to share and I don't have to return things." She knows me well enough to know that I would not agree to her request.

She pulled out the bags from the sari store and informed me that instead of two saris and two Indian suits, there were about eight extra saris. Turns out that when Sadhna was in the store and saying no, the person to the side misunderstood and wound up putting everything into bags. I did some quick calculations and exchange rate conversions and discovered we had an extra $450 worth of clothing we did not pay for. My response was immediate: "We have to go back." Fortunately, I had a business card from them and they were not too far from our hotel. A quick cup of tea and we were ready to go out. Sadhna knew that it was the right thing to do, but you could tell she was torn.

We picked up the bags and made our way outside. The streets were full of litter, there were piles of garbage, the walls were dirty, and the smells were distinct: rotting food, urine, and a slight odour of incense. I couldn't understand how anything as beautiful as the Taj Mahal could be in such a dismal setting. We had been in electric and low-emission vehicles because the officials want to limit the environmental destruction that could impact the Taj Mahal, and yet this was one of the dirtiest and smelliest places that I have experienced. The low-emission vehicles might go some way to protecting the Taj

Mahal, but it is a very small gesture that has little or no effect on the overall problem of air, water, and noise pollution. The Taj Mahal is a jewel floating in a sea of waste.

When we reached the store, I informed the owner that there had been a mistake and to not get mad at the staff member because it was a simple error. We showed him the goods and his eyes widened. He thanked us for being honest and we said our goodbyes. We trudged back to our hotel, dodging the filth, and all the while Sadhna was saying, "He could have at least given us something for being honest." I was indifferent. After a rest, we made our way to the dining room to get our dinner and called it an early evening.

Before the day ended, I ventured out to an Internet café in a shack beside our hotel: one computer, one table, and one chair, all in a space a little bigger than the average washroom—but the Internet connection was so fast. I had a cup of tea and managed to share some of my adventures to date.

This day had shown us some of the best and the worst that India had to offer. I didn't think I wanted to see any more of Agra, but the Taj Mahal was certainly a highlight of the trip so far. There was such a contrast of beauty and unpleasantness: vibrancy and colour amidst poverty and busyness.

India to this point had certainly not been a vacation, but it was definitely an experience. It was difficult to find moments of solitude, and it felt as if we were always on the go. To be fair, that might just reflect the tour we had booked, but I think all of my senses were overwhelmed. I don't think one can prepare for India. Until you are standing in it, you can't begin to understand the poverty, noise, and crowding. Where was I on the traveller–tourist spectrum? Was I a traveller, trying to embrace and appreciate what was before me, both good and bad, and make it into an experience that penetrated me, or was I a tourist who was out to sightsee and just check mark what I saw? I can say confidently that India was not easy and I was trying to travel with an open mind. I was being elevated to new experiences that I had never even imagined, and which were beginning to shake me to the core. India was like no other place I had ever visited. I decided I was a traveller.

12

MAKING OUR WAY ALONG THE GOLDEN SAMOSA

*Fatehpur Sikri |
Jal Mahal | Amer Fort |
Hawa Mahal |
Jaipur City Palace |
Jantar Mantar*

THE NEXT MORNING, we got up early for the trip to Jaipur. They call this area the Golden Triangle because Delhi, Agra, and Jaipur form a triangle. I think I would rather refer to it as the Golden Samosa. Is that not a more fitting name?

As we made our way to the lobby for breakfast, the silence was broken by a man playing a sarangi, an instrument that looks a bit like a violin. He was tall, with a bright-red tunic and turban and white churidars (tight white pants that are traditional with this type of outfit). He had a Rajasthani-style moustache, long and waxed at the tips. Sikhs tie their turban so that it has neat pleats and is very tight. Oftentimes, Sikhs' turbans are very plain and not loud. The Rajasthani turban, however, is much brighter, vibrant, and wrapped around, so that no two turbans are exactly alike. They also let a piece of cloth trail out of the turban so it drapes to mid-back. A boy about five years old next to him was nicely dressed and adorned like the man, so they may have been a father–son team. As the man played, the boy moved in a traditional dance between the tables. His hands were waving and circling and his head would go side to side. As he came towards us, he smiled and continued to dance gracefully. Sadhna found a few rupee notes for the child.

I thought the music and dancing were beautiful, but shouldn't this boy have been in school? What would happen to him as he grew older and was no longer a cute, baby-faced dancer? These questions swirled around in my head much like my thoughts about poverty at Jama Masjid, but the man and boy did not look destitute.

After breakfast, we strolled through a park and back to the Taj Mahal for about an hour. I felt I needed to gaze upon its magnificence one more time, as I might never again have this opportunity. We wandered about, and the guides and photographers approached us like hungry ducks in a park. I think I would have paid someone to create a sign saying, "Do not disturb us as we walk." Before leaving, I turned one last time to gaze upon the site before we headed back to the hotel. While walking, we occasionally stopped to watch a monkey approach an unsuspecting victim and steal part of their meal before making a break for the nearest tree. This was our morning's entertainment.

We were checked out and on the road by 10:30 a.m., with just Narendra. We drove for about thirty kilometres and came to an area atop a hill. There, with a frantic wave, was Nasser. He greeted us as we pulled up. As we got out, I could see that the area was arid, and I could feel a dry heat. There was a bit of a refreshing breeze. We stood there admiring the distant hills.

Nasser began telling us about the town of Fatehpur Sikri and how it was built in the 16th century by the Mughal emperor Akbar. It was in very good condition and the structures looked as though they had hardly been used. Nasser explained that it was conceived as a new city, but they had underestimated the required water supply this high up and, as a result, the site was soon abandoned. I guess some things never change: not all projects have the best processes in place.

As we explored the rooms, I felt a gush of air on the back of my neck. Nasser explained that part of the reason these structures were built atop a hill was because of the breeze, and if we had a careful look, we would see an almost hollow section between the walls. The breeze would catch the large open window area above us, go down a chamber and into the room, where it would be breezy. At times the air could also be cooled further by water in the area, like an old-school air conditioner. They had such engineering magic back then.

The story is that a saint lived in this area and blessed Akbar with a son. In gratitude, Akbar built this city on top of the mountain. The entire area is in sandstone and has a red, earthy tone. We walked into the room holding the marble tomb of the saint and paid our respects.

Then we were on the road again, starting on a long journey of about 250 kilometres to Jaipur. We passed fields, towns, and people. We took it all in and appreciated the life that surrounded us as we continued to drive. I was present in the moment, but also thinking more and more about looking for my village and roots. *What if I don't find it? What if I do find it? How will we be received? What will we say?* I pulled out my map of India and looked at the area of the Punjab. It was going to be a challenging search, because I didn't have much information and this was a huge country with a lot of people. I closed my book and put it in my backpack and continued to gaze at the landscape. The gentle swaying and rocking of the car compelled me to put my head back, and I fell into a light sleep.

I am not quite sure how long I slept, but when I opened my eyes, I saw that traffic had picked up. Nasser broke the silence to inform us that we were entering Jaipur but that we would see the city tomorrow. It had been a long drive and we could go to our hotel now and relax. As we neared the hotel, which was just outside Jaipur, there was a lake to our right and the hotel across the street on our left. The lake had a stillness to it, and out in the middle of it, was an abandoned summer palace called Jal Mahal and its mirrored reflection in the water. Again, I marvelled at the engineering wonders from back in the day, how this Rajput symmetrical structure was created in the midst of a lake.

We pulled into the long driveway of the Trident Hotel and saw that it was quite a nice-looking, modern place. We checked in, and even though it was only mid-afternoon, we decided to stay there and enjoy the hotel. Closer to sunset, I walked down the driveway to the lake. While the palace still shimmered in the stillness of the water, upon closer inspection I saw the water was murky and thick, like watered-down hot chocolate. Rubbish littered the shore and there was a musty, pungent smell. As the sun began to set, though, the debris and muddy shores seemed to disappear into the picturesque glow of the golden sun on the palace. The site was transformed for a while into a regal elegance as the surroundings slowly grew darker. The palace faded into the background until it was only a shadow. As it disappeared, I felt I should make my way back up the driveway to relax.

We sat by the pool, ordered chai, and savoured it while listening to the chirping birds signalling the end of the day. Bliss. I finally felt I could catch my breath after our luggage fiasco, and the full days of driving and sightseeing.

The next morning, I got up early, when it was still dark outside. The room had a tea-making service, so I brewed a cup and sat there in the darkness. Wherever I am in the world, I find such comfort in sipping a hot cup of tea. It provides the calming sense I need to start my day. The birds began chirping again, which meant that dawn was upon us. I enjoyed the last few drops of tea, grabbed my camera, and headed out to the lake across the road to capture some sunrise photos. As I stood there in the darkness, facing the lake and the shadowy outline of the palace I had left last night, the sky started to glow orange on the horizon and things began coming back to life. Little ripples appeared in the water as fish broke the surface, looking for their morning meal.

The odd vehicle passed on the highway behind me, breaking the silence. The sweet sound of the birds chimed in every so often to welcome the morning. I had one of those Canon film cameras, not a fancy digital SLR. With film, you never know what you've captured, and when you get it developed you hope there is a decent image amongst all those you've taken. With different apertures, angles, and settings, there had to be one decent image, my own *National Geographic* shot!

The sun peeked from behind the mountains and then lumbered higher and higher with every passing moment, and the shades of orange grew brighter and brighter. I shot an entire roll of film because the shadows and shades kept shifting and changing. I started to feel the welcome of a new day as the sun cast its warm glow on the summer palace and it came to life once more.

A blaring, echoing sound disturbed the quietness of the morning. It was the call to prayer that Muslims around the world hear a number of times each day. It was a sound I had heard in Fiji many years back and now encountered only on TV or in movies, and it made me think about far-off places, but here I was, listening to the prayers and thinking how exotic it was. I closed my eyes and heard the words. I did not understand them, but it was a sweet sound that penetrated the air. Satisfied, I put the cap back on the lens and crossed the road, which had already started to buzz with traffic, and entered our room just as Sadhna was waking up. She had no idea I had slipped out and had been gone for an hour.

After breakfast, and with a bit of time before we'd be picked up by Narendra, we decided to go poolside one more time and have a relaxing cup of chai. It was such a tranquil place to watch the birds swoop in, sit by the pool, bathe, and chirp.

We went and met the car. Today, we were going to explore Jaipur. I had heard much about this city, which is often referred to as the Pink City because the structures are either in pink sandstone or painted pink. Narendra and Nasser greeted us with the customary "Namaste" and with that, we were whisked away. While we waited for a break in traffic so we could pull out, an elephant trundled past the driveway. This was Jaipur traffic? After the elephant went past, we were able to enter the artery of traffic, but it was not as busy as Delhi or Agra.

We went left, to Amer Fort. Nasser said we would save the Pink City for later in the day. I glanced over to the lake and could now see the summer palace in daylight. It was no longer masked by the morning light or by darkness, and it looked neglected and less brilliant in plain view.

I started thinking about my journey and what had brought me to India. I still had my daunting task ahead of me. I considered how people either did not know where the village was or had never heard of it, and that even if we by some remote chance should find it, we would need to be prepared for a mixed reception. Was this a good idea? If I was successful in finding the village and my roots, I might upset a lot of people. Would they ask us, how come you never came this way before? Would they say that we were no longer part of this village? I was still a foreigner in a land that should not be foreign to me. I was an observer trying to appreciate and understand this chaotic country. Being on a journey with no guarantee of success causes you to doubt yourself. It is a sort of mental battle of obstacles and opportunities, possibilities over challenges. I told myself that I would face those challenges and questions if we made it to the village, and focused on our next stop: Amer Fort.

As we got out, I looked up at the top of this small hill and saw a magnificent structure perched along a windy pathway. It is called Amer Fort, but it reminded me of a palace as well. The outer walls were akin to a fortified garrison, and behind the massive walls was the palace. Amer was the capital of the princely Jaipur state. Amer Fort was constructed between the late 1500s and early 1600s, and is a blend of Rajput (Hindu) and Mughal (Islamic) design. Centuries ago it was inhabited by maharajas, but it now sits as a World Heritage Site.

Nasser directed us to the gates and then we were through and standing at the base area with other tourists. He showed us the mode of transport we would use to get up the hill. Elephant power! A number of elephants were carrying tourists up the hill, in a type of elephant train. We walked up a set of wooden stairs to a platform, and before we knew it, we were slowly rocking back and forth on this magnificent, brightly adorned creature. We sat sidesaddle in the comfort of a low open box. Every step raised us a few inches so we could see more of the view. I slipped my hand down between the cloth material to the elephant's tough, wrinkly hide. The elephant just went about its duty, leading us through massive doors and into a courtyard.

TOP Early morning sunrise over the summer palace—one of my favourite places to welcome the new day.

BOTTOM The Hawa Mahal stood before us. The intricate work of sandstone windows was one of the main features of Jaipur.

Riding the elephant made me think I would rather walk next time, as this mode of transport seemed like a touristy thing to do. I wanted to experience a grounding sort of understanding to satisfy my curiosity, to make it more of a journey. Tours showcase the beauty of the country, but I also wanted to recognize the blemishes and challenges. I wanted to be shown the good and the bad, and to see how they blend to make this country a colourful mosaic. Riding elephants or observing carpet-making is what tourists do, and I wanted something more meaningful and powerful. I wanted to be moved.

Nasser was waiting for us in the courtyard when we dismounted on the second level of the fort. The elephant went on its way to pick up more passengers, like a carnival amusement ride. We were led into the walls of the fort and observed that this structure had seen better days. Shrubs had taken hold on various areas of the stone walls in the courtyard, and there were chunks of concrete showing beneath the surface walls. As we walked along the inner walls, we saw colourful mosaics with missing tesserae that had been poked out and likely taken home as souvenirs. The richness and opulence of this place had faded over the years. What had once been a bustling and thriving community was now an empty shell filled with tourists. What was it like to live in the era, I wondered.

Exploring the site allowed me to find small, intricate details such as the stone latticework or the ceiling with tiny pieces of mirror glistening down upon me. Every so often I ran my hands along the wall and came across someone's writing in Hindi scribbled or etched as they walked along the corridor. Small graffiti letterings had been etched in English and Hindi into the sandstone walls along corridors, announcing the love between young souls—*Jas loves Tina*; *Rishi* + *Vidya*; and so on. I stopped Sadhna every so often and asked her to interpret. Most times they were just names scribbled by individuals who were more interested in leaving their mark than in appreciating the treasure they were seeing.

We meandered through the corridors and wound up outside again. This time we walked down the hill, manoeuvring between the people and elephants coming up. People sat by the side of the path and sold trinkets. One lady in particular caught my eye. She was wearing a rich, beautiful red shawl draped over her head. She held out an attractive *mala* (necklace) of vibrant orange marigolds and red carnations. It was as if someone had dipped the flowers in bright paints. She smiled, so I reached down and gave her some of my rupees and she handed over the garland for Sadhna in a shy way, so Sadhna could use it in prayers later that day. Just a small gesture, and we parted with a smile but no words.

With that, we were back in the car and on our way to the Pink City. The bustle of life formed around us again as we neared Jaipur. Sure enough, it was pink all around. The city seemed to be better laid out than Agra, and definitely cleaner. We drove past the Hawa Mahal, a palace with just under a thousand windows. *Hawa* means wind in Hindi, and *mahal* means palace; the wind would come in through these windows and cool the palace.

We visited other sites, including the City Palace, which still houses the modern-day raj or prince. We passed through the city archway a few times, which looked weathered, as we darted about, in and around the city.

For me, one of the most interesting stops was Jantar Mantar, which contains a collection of outdoor astronomical structures. There was a massive sundial that agreed with my watch. In other displays, the structures outline the position of the moon, planets, and celestial bodies. I walked about and tried to really appreciate the magnitude of what I was experiencing. Brilliant minds used science and Sanskrit to create this place, without the aid of computers. They were forward thinkers and built something that was meant to help humanity better understand our place in the universe. To me, it was more than a tourist stop; it showed me the ingenuity and skills required to create magnificence.

Astronomy has always been a keen interest of mine, as I like to lie outside staring at the stars and wondering about our existence. I wandered and wondered, and after an hour Nasser said it was time to go. I pointed to the massive sundial and said, "Stand here, look at the sundial, and give me fifteen more minutes." He smiled and nodded, and I explored the grounds. Eventually, I came back and he pointed to the sundial, said, "You were gone for seventeen minutes, sir," and smiled again. With that, we headed back to the car and our hotel.

After a lovely dinner, we went for a walk. It was only about a kilometre there and back to the shops, and it was starting to get dark out, but the nightlife was just beginning to emerge. Roadside stalls became more visible with embers glowing inside them. You could smell cooking that was heavy with ghee. The cooks were proudly making their sweets or savoury items. There were groups of people all around talking and walking, looking for just the right meal and conversation. Cars passed, and their headlights cut a path so we could make out the store in the near distance and the hotel behind us. The summer palace started to disappear back into its cloak of darkness.

13

NOT EVERYTHING IS WHAT IT SEEMS

Chandni Chowk

WHAT DOES ONE do when lying awake at 4 a.m.? Make a cup of tea, go to the armchair, turn on a small light so as not to wake up your wife, and begin to read. I picked up my book on India from the side table and read about some of the places we had been thus far and about where we would be going. I also pulled out my journal and reflected on what I had written so far. I wound up drifting in and out of the words and the world I had been experiencing. I read a little, looked blankly at the wall, and images appeared to me.

I wondered what life was like for my ancestors, and the type of legacy I wanted to leave for my family. I grew up living my life but not really appreciating those who had come before me. There is my physical DNA and then there is my cultural DNA. Physical DNA is *what* you are and cultural DNA is *who* you are. Cultural DNA is who I am with regards to my morals, values, and ethics. We assume a cultural DNA by the influences around us, but where do these aspects come from? I needed to better understand and appreciate my cultural DNA. For me to be complete, I had to imagine my past in order to prepare for the future while standing on this crack I call the present.

The first week had been an interesting one. I came to this country as a foreigner, and while I still felt like only an observer, I was picking up some of the intricacies of what it means to be Indian. I appreciated how genuine people were with us, and how many people were content with their lot in life. India had already been like no other country I had visited, and we were thankful for the protective care of our guardians: our driver and guides. I was learning more and more about this country, its food, and its people. I didn't think it would be possible for me ever to be a local, but slowly I was finding my sense of place. I was starting to realize that I was not just a tourist, but a curious bystander who was open to experiences.

While shopping at a marketplace in Jaipur, I had purchased another map that unfolded to show the state of Punjab. This was where I needed to go. It was not a detailed map, and would not make my journey any easier, but I think it was a comfort purchase that I needed to add to my growing supplies in an effort to find my village.

Running my fingers along the map, I traced our next week of travel to the Punjab. Somewhere out there lay our village. Somewhere in the vastness of the Punjab was my goal. Would I realize it? It looked like a daunting task.

Nonetheless, I was determined. Failure was not an option for me, but the circumstances might dictate otherwise. I would not let self-doubt about the odds and time hold me back from at least trying. Instead of thinking about not reaching my goal, I reflected on what I would do when I found the village. I held on to the flicker of what might be and kept fuelling it so that it burned brighter and brighter. I reminded myself why this was so important to me: if I didn't find my roots and we skipped another generation, the village would be lost forever from our family history, and that was something I was not comfortable with. Sure, I could trace my origins to the Punjab, but I wanted to pinpoint them and attach them to a specific place and not to the vastness of an entire state.

I reached for my tea and realized it had cooled while I was busy concentrating and contemplating. The disappointment was short-lived, as I made a fresh cup.

The following week, we would visit the Punjab. We'd go from Delhi to Amritsar, Amritsar to Jalandhar, and then Jalandhar to Delhi, with the latter part of the trip set aside to seek out my village. It seemed easy enough to trace on a map, but the details were not too accurate and I was not quite sure where some of the key markers were; plus, I had only a limited amount of information. I reached into the pocket of my journal and pulled out the photo of the people from our village one more time and looked closely at their faces. The photo was old and faded, but I was hopeful that some of the people in the photo were still around. I felt as if I was close and distant at the same time. I thought to myself, *What are they doing right now?* Well, likely sleeping, but was there even a glimmer of my presence as they slept? They were very prominent in my world, as an image, but they were unaware of my existence at this point. I sipped my tea, savoured its comfort, and pondered this thought.

Our next week would be with a new driver who was local to the Punjab and might be able to support us in our search. For now, we appreciated the Golden Triangle and all that it had shown us. I don't think I have ever had such a rich and overwhelming experience in my life. It seems as though, with India, you can't slow down to appreciate what it holds. You are always on the go, and you collect your experiences as you move along, like shopping in a supermarket and putting items into your grocery cart without reading the ingredients. You pick up memories and capture impressions with your senses, and then you put it all away to think about later.

I glanced at my watch. It was now 6 a.m., time for us to get up and return to Delhi, closing out the first week of travel.

The journey from Jaipur to Delhi was fairly quiet. Nasser had bid us farewell yesterday at the hotel, and every so often Narendra would glance back and smile, as we would be parting ways in Delhi.

On the outskirts of the city, Narendra pulled over at a roadside stall. It was a small open-air structure made of concrete. The plaster was worn out and dirty with soot from all the years of frying and cooking. As Narendra walked up to the owner, it was obvious that he knew him. They shook hands and Narendra talked to him, pointed to us, and smiled. We were at an Indian sweet shop and the owner was making jalebi, a very sweet deep-fried treat that is crispy on the outside and syrupy within. I was used to having them made very thinly, about the circumference of a doughnut, with the cook swirling the mix and then dropping the batter in a constant stream into boiling oil. The designs are butterfly shapes or swirls that instantly harden as they hit the oil, so that when you take a bite, the crispiness crackles and the syrup inside gushes out. The ones I saw outside Delhi were different. They were actually quite large, the size and width of a steering wheel, with raisins. I think Narendra wanted to get one for us, but as he went to pick one up, the owner waved a cloth and the raisins flew away. Yes, the raisins were flies! We quickly said that we were full, and no thank you. Narendra smiled, bobbed his head from side to side, and we were soon driving into the arteries of Delhi. We did not want to disrespect our host and driver, but this was something we thought was not going to be safe.

Finally, we pulled into our next hotel, called the Janpath, about 3 p.m. This hotel was at the heart of Delhi and was listed as a business person's hotel. Sounds good enough, right? As we pulled up the driveway, there was something about this place that was unlike the other places we had stayed. No one was neatly dressed to greet us at the door with their hands drawn together.

So Narendra helped us with our bags and we shook hands, hugged, and said our goodbyes. We knew that our lives would never cross again. Narendra drove off in his Ambassador, and we walked into the lobby of the Janpath Hotel and up to the front desk.

The man behind the desk was dressed nicely and glanced up at us. For some reason, the look from him was not of welcome, as one would expect, but rather the arrogance of an aristocrat. As I handed him our reservation, he checked his box file and then looked back up at us to inform me that there was no reservation under our name. There was no "Sorry" or "Let's see what happened." It was more like, "There is no reservation, thank you." And we were a minor inconvenience. It felt like a scene out of *Fawlty Towers*, and he was John Cleese but not that funny to us. I asked him to look again. He started to get aggressive and a bit rude, and told us there was no reservation. We went back and forth as I showed him the confirmation number and told him that I had even called the night before from Jaipur. Still, he was not going to back down. Finally, after looking further, he found the reservation. They had us staying for two nights. Without a word of apology, he gave us a key. I told him that we were going to spend one night here and then head to the Punjab the next day. He shrugged his shoulders and looked at our reservation again and said that we were down for one night now and one night upon our return next week. So I confirmed with him that it was only one night for now, and he said, "It looks like it."

A park in Delhi offered a moment of respite.

Afterwards, I decided to phone our booking agent to make sure we were only here for this one night. They confirmed this, and it had also been confirmed by the front desk person. As I walked to the elevator, it dawned on me that perhaps he was looking for some *bakshi* (bribe) to find the booking that was already there, and when we did not relent, he had to give up.

The foyer of the Janpath Hotel was well lit, with glistening marble floors, but that was where the opulence ended. The elevator had a worn-out carpet and was big enough to accommodate only four people. As the door opened on our floor, we found ourselves standing outside on a long balcony, with doors to the rooms running along one side, like a motel. The doors all looked old and weathered. Our door, at the end of the corridor, opened to reveal a room that was dark, old, and dingy— nothing like the ones we had experienced thus far. The chairs were faded and crushed by years of use. The bedsheets were grey and not very clean. I walked into the bathroom, and the large tub and sink had years of accumulated stains.

I looked at Sadhna and she looked at me, and we felt like leaving this place immediately. But we decided to make the one night work and then take off to the Ambassador Hotel when we returned from the Punjab. Comparing the images on the website with what was before us, we had to concede that the reality didn't live up to our expectations. I went online and reserved the familiar and comfortable Ambassador Hotel and sighed with relief. Sure, it was more expensive, but you could not put a price on comfort versus the confrontation we'd just endured. After reluctantly using the shower, I felt more refreshed and realized I was embarking on perhaps the most difficult part of the journey: shopping with my wife!

We had seen and experienced much, but now the time had come to get serious. We needed some professional help, or else every shopkeeper would take full advantage of us, no matter how hard we haggled. Fortunately, a dear friend in Canada had a niece, Shilpa, who lived in Delhi. She was assigned to protect us from deceptive shopkeepers. We had been assured of her credentials as a master-level shopper who would go toe to toe with any salesperson.

Shilpa met us at the hotel in a taxi. She arrived with a smile and hugs. It felt as if this was the first time we had been greeted with the warmth of a family member. That was short-lived, however, as she looked to Sadhna with tactical precision and asked what she needed. Sadhna gave her the list. I could see Shilpa doing the logistics and then she turned to Karan, the taxi driver, and with confidence and authority pointed forward and said that we needed to get to Chandni Chowk, one of the busiest marketplaces in India.

When we reached Chandni Chowk, Karan pulled over and Shilpa got out of the taxi and gave him further instructions. I saw a myriad of buildings that were jumbled together like a poorly constructed Lego city. Signs about soaps, the latest Hindi movies, and miracle cures were posted in every available spot. Complicated bundles of wires strung between the buildings only about ten feet above the ground looked like serious fire hazards. Some large, overloaded carts were being pushed or pulled by skinny brown men. They had on wraparound cloths called dhotis, and undershirts. Some wearing sandals and some barefoot, they heaved on their heavy loads and dared not stop for fear the momentum might knock them over. They looked as if they wouldn't have been capable of shifting a chair, so their tremendous strength and stamina impressed me as their loads looked to be five to ten times their weight. Looking at the overloaded carts, I thought surely they would touch the overhead wiring or the cargo would fall onto unsuspecting shoppers below. Faded awnings covered with a layer of dust offered some shelter for shoppers. People were coming and going from all directions; some were there to shop, while others were just chatting with their friends. Cars, carts, and bikes were weaving between the people. It all looked so confusing, a mishmash of anything and everything.

It was Tuesday, so the market should not be too busy, explained Shilpa. We were in search of shawls and needed about nine of them. I found the marketplace to be a maze. We would walk along and then make an abrupt turn, go farther and make another abrupt turn, on and on. Shilpa walked with determination, glancing back at us to make sure we were still accounted for.

There were small tents and stalls and some side buildings. Some stalls were open to the air, with very little covering, while others offered more goods and looked like mini department stores. Everything was laid out for you to inspect and was very specialized. We walked past a spice stall. Baskets of spices were laid out, with many different colours painting a culinary rainbow. I stopped to take a photo but saw that Shilpa was not stopping, so I snapped a quick shot and carried on. A few steps further was a store selling shiny metal cookware, followed by a food stall offering fresh pakoras.

I had no idea where we were. It was like entering a thick forest and losing all sense of direction because you cannot make out any reference points. Like a well-trusted guide, Shilpa snaked her way through the streets. She was on a mission: she knew what she wanted and where to get it. After many twists and turns, we went into an old building and I had to bend down to avoid hitting my head. Then we climbed a rickety set of stairs to the second floor. It was dark, and we walked past a few more stalls. Finally, we came to a doorway and walked in.

Shilpa said hello to the shopkeeper. They knew each other. He had on a dhoti and a white dress shirt. He was thin, balding, and had on wire-rimmed glasses. He seemed seasoned in his trade. We all sat on the floor on pads with white sheets, Shilpa near the shopkeeper, Sadhna just behind her and to the side, while I blended into the darkness and wall behind them all. The shopkeeper summoned his aide and asked us what we wanted to drink. "Chai, soda, *pani* [water]?" A nice chai sounded perfect.

With a flick of hands, spotlights came on and there behind him were walls of shawls. Wow! Where would we start? I felt as if I was in a casino and the shopkeeper was the card dealer and Shilpa the gambler. Shilpa turned to Sadhna, and Sadhna described what she needed. I enjoyed how I did not even factor into the discussion, and was able to just sit quietly in the background with my legs crossed and watch with interest. The shopkeeper nodded and pulled off about six different shawls to start, laying each one before Sadhna. She pointed to one or two of them and said what she liked and did not like, helping to narrow the search. Sadhna asked how much they cost and was immediately hushed by the shopkeeper, who said, "Don't worry, I give you good price," with what I felt was a sly and clever look.

Eventually, we had a pile of about nine shawls. Shilpa put her hand on them and turned to Sadhna for approval of the purchases, and Sadhna nodded in agreement. "Now we decide on the price?" asked Sadhna.

Shilpa shifted position, straightened herself up, and folded her arms in preparation for the haggling battle. It was like watching two prizefighters ready to go at each other and waiting for the bell to ring. In a casual voice, Shilpa asked the shopkeeper to name his price.

Round 1: He looked at the goods, lifted them up, studied them carefully, and then wrote some numbers on a slip of paper. He handed the slip of paper to Shilpa.

Round 2: She looked at the paper and threw her hands in the air. She pointed at the shopkeeper and then to us and told him how we could have gone anywhere but had chosen his place and that the price was too high.

She took a pen and scratched out his number and wrote a new one. The slip of paper was thrust back to the shopkeeper.

Round 3: He looked at the paper and put his palms to his forehead and shook his head from side to side in disbelief. His tone of voice raised as he now pointed behind himself at his goods and told her that he was making a meagre living and that it was very difficult to run the business and look after his family. He took the piece of paper, scratched out her offer, and proceeded to write a new number. He pushed it back to her for approval.

Round 4: She took the paper and looked at it. Now her hand went to her heart and she looked down, closed her eyes, and shook her head. She leaned closer to him and now her voice was raised. In a very abrupt tone and pointing at him, she was telling him how he was taking advantage of us. That she knew he had marked up the prices. She pointed to us, saying we were family to her and not just anyone who showed up in his shop. She took the piece of paper and scratched off the last price and shoved it back to the shopkeeper abruptly.

Round 5: The shopkeeper looked at the slip of paper and angrily threw it down. He leaned forward and said it was insulting that she felt his shop and his goods were not worthy. It was customers like us who were making it very difficult for him to feed his family and that was why they were suffering. He pointed to a picture of a family, maybe his, to show how much he was a family man. He picked up the piece of paper and wrote a new number and threw it over to Shilpa.

Round 6: Now Shilpa seemed to be equally agitated. I thought they were going to get into a heated argument that would escalate into very bad feelings. She took the paper, wrote down a number, and said it was the final offer, and with that, she forcibly handed him the paper and threw the pencil to the ground. She clapped her hands as in, "We are done!"

Round 7: He took it, looked up at her through his glasses, and extended his hand to her. Like that, it was over. There had been a shouting match and it almost looked as if they were on the brink of a relationship meltdown, and now they were shaking hands, sipping tea, and asking for news of their respective families. This was not shopping, it was an art form!

Satisfied, we went to leave with our goods, with me handing over all the rupee notes to pay for the admission to this event. The shopkeeper picked up one of the discarded shawls and gave it to Shilpa, the usual practice to show gratitude to a customer for helping the business.

We now proceeded to another area of Chandni Chowk to see saris. There was a repeat of the same match. This played out a few times, and before we knew it, our shopping in Chandni Chowk was done, so we grabbed some lunch, surrounded by about nine bags of clothing. Shilpa manoeuvred us through the alleyways of stalls back to our taxi and driver.

We went to a couple more sari stores that were on a large scale, spread over multiple floors. I was amazed that you could have a sari department store. One shop even had a rickety old elevator, and as the door opened, an old man seated on a stool looked at us. Shilpa gave a floor number and he pushed the button. We got to the floor and the doors opened to a colourful room full of saris. A few more purchases and we were done, and the elevator came back and the old man pushed another button and we were going down. As we left the elevator, I wondered how long he had been doing this job. There must be more to life than pushing an elevator button all day and only seeing the door to the world open and close in front of you. However, he was working and earning something for his family. The least I could do was to shake his hand as I left, and that put a smile on the old man's face.

Shilpa had accomplished her task, and now it was time to head back to our hotel and try to enjoy our not so comfortable room. We said goodbye to Shilpa, and proceeded into the lobby, the elevator, and along the outside corridor to our door. Sadhna always carried bedsheets from home, and this was one of the few times I asked to use one. Despite all our challenges with the Janpath Hotel, this was probably one of the most restful sleeps I had while in India—whether from the added security of a chair placed under the door handle or because I was so tired from the journey the day before. Another day complete, and the next morning we would start to the North, and the Punjab.

14

THE MOST
EXHAUSTING
ROAD

---

*New Delhi
to Amritsar*

I WAS ABOUT TO enter the area of India where my ancestral roots are located. The tourist hat, or turban in this case, was going to be replaced by the deeper and more experiential part of the journey. I don't think anything about the Punjab portion was really structured as sightseeing. Delhi and the Golden Triangle were more in line with any association I had with India, because they were more mainstream and I could speak the language to some extent. In the Punjab, they speak a language I am not fluent in. While I would be disconnected from the language and customs, there was an inner feeling that drew me towards this place.

The Punjab region is north of Delhi and we would be spending just under a week there. Apart from the search for my village, there was an important landmark that I had to see. The holy capital for Sikhs is Amritsar, with its Golden Temple. I am Sikh by birth, by ancestry, and by name, and while I am not orthodox, I hoped that if I visited there first, some divine intervention might help me find my roots in Hoshiarpur.

For this second leg of our journey, we had booked Raja as a driver. Even though he was from the Punjab, he had never heard of our village and was not familiar with the area where our village might be. Raja arrived the next morning as arranged and was in the lobby of the Janpath Hotel waiting for us. He was tall and of slender build. He wore Western clothes and seemed relaxed and casual. He also looked younger than any of the drivers and guides to date. I reached out and shook his hand. I then turned around and restated to the new gentleman at the front desk that we were not going to be back and that I wanted to confirm that we had booked only the one night. I got a verbal confirmation, but a small part of me was still not sure he fully understood. It was like he was saying, "Yes, yes, no problem, sir," but really he had no idea what I was talking about. Technically, everything indicated that our bookings were in order, but I had a gut feeling that all was not as easy as it seemed. One thing I had learned about India is that things are chaotic but at the same time there is a level of order and things do get done. I am not sure how, but things do get done ... except there was a level of doubt in this case.

As we stepped outside, the air was heavy with smog. A thick coat of smoke hung in the air from the fires that started the morning routines for the people in the area. There was another fellow standing by the vehicle. Turns out that Tony (a good solid Sikh name) was Raja's friend and was going to accompany us. Raja and Tony had driven down from the Punjab yesterday and spent the night in Delhi so that they could be here early to pick us up. I noticed that our vehicle was a four-by-four and not an Ambassador. The road to Amritsar was long, and having a four-by-four would allow us to be perched higher and somehow feel a bit safer; however, again, there were no seat belts. It was a boxy sort of vehicle and relatively new, adorned with bobbles and trinkets. There was carpeting on the ceiling and lights—it looked like a Bedouin tent.

We loaded our luggage in the back and took our positions and were off, leaving the Janpath Hotel behind. Once we were on the road, we realized that Raja might not know how to leave Delhi. We drove around a bit and every so often he would pull up to someone and ask for directions. Raja would be driving and then Tony would say, "I think that way," and then we we'd go down another road, which meant pulling over and someone trying to direct us back. I felt like a ball in a pinball machine being bounced around. With so much Delhi traffic, it is challenging to change lanes or get into a roundabout. Eventually, though, we found the road and then it was smooth sailing.

Once we got out of the heart of Delhi, the traffic eased up and the roads became straighter. Raja could make out my Hindi, so we would converse. Every so often Sadhna would have to jump in to further explain what I was trying to say. I found that when she said things, the words just flowed and I could see the expressions on the faces of the people she was talking to, giving an understanding nod as they realized what I had been struggling to express.

After a couple of hours we pulled into a *dhaba*, where Raja and Tony joined us for lunch. I looked over the menu and saw maki roti (corn roti) and saag (a greenish curry made from a mixture of greens) with dahi (yogurt). On top of the saag was a massive helping of ghee (clarified butter), and it all just melted and blended together. As I was nearing the last bite of my roti, the owner came over and plopped down another one. As I was eating it and starting to get full, he came by and dropped another one. I had to put up my hand and tell him to stop or he would have just kept making fresh rotis.

After we ate, a gentleman came by with rolled-up papers, which turned out to be maps. I asked if he had one of the Punjab. He unravelled it and showed me. "Okay, I will take that one. How much?" The seller looked at me almost like a carnival weight guesser. He blurted out 50 rupees, or almost $1.50 Canadian. I was about to pay, but Raja jumped in and said no, really, how much, and next thing I knew, he had negotiated the price down to 10 rupees, or 30 cents. I felt a bit bad giving the man only 10 rupees when I was prepared to give 50, so I slid him an extra 10. It was not a lot of money, but with this act I knew I was not Indian.

I looked carefully at the map. It was printed on two sides, and was about twenty-four inches by thirty inches.

I found the district of Jalandhar and then the district of Hoshiarpur. Hoshiarpur—this is where our village is! While I was searching with my finger, I stopped abruptly and brought the map closer to my face. I had found Garhshankar on the map! This meant that our search now had about a ten-kilometre radius. This was the first time I felt that the possibilities were overcoming the challenges. Was it possible that somewhere in that ten-kilome-tre zone lay my quest to discover my ancestral roots? At least we had narrowed it down to an area where the haystack might be, but it was still a very large haystack.

Before we took off, I leaned forward and shared the map with Raja and Tony, pointing to approximately where we needed to go. Just like in the movies, where the lieutenant shares the mission with his troops, I cir-cled Garhshankar with a pen and a satisfying level of confidence. The map was somewhat detailed, but not enough to show Jandoli or other villages. I felt I was getting closer and closer to what I was in India to find.

The journey to Amritsar from Delhi was 450 kilome-tres. We drove and drove, and every so often we'd pull over to stretch. Towns passed by and began blending into one another to a point where it felt as if we were just moving around in a large circle. We would slow down as traffic thickened with all sorts of vehicles, and I glanced about and saw plaster buildings where daily businesses were taking place, *dhabas* to the side of the road with plastic chairs and tables inviting passersby for tea, peo-ple of all sorts going about their daily lives, trying to eke out a meagre living.

A simple meal in a *dhaba* kept us going on many legs of the journey.

The kilometres passed at a slow pace and so did the time, and as it began to get darker, we found there was fog forming, which got thicker and thicker and just seemed to hang in place. Eventually, Raja pulled into a rest area and said that it was getting dangerous to drive. I could see why, as I had never been in fog this thick before. If you used the headlights, you could barely see ahead, and if you used your high beams, it was as if your lights were hitting a white wall barely one foot in front of you. Raja was speaking with the other drivers who had also pulled into the rest area. Perhaps if they formed a convoy of sorts, using each other's lights and hazard lights as beacons, this could work.

One by one, the drivers got back into their cars and we slowly proceeded along the highway. Like a flock of geese in formation, with headlights on low beam and hazard lights blinking, we moved in unison. Traffic was slow and meandering, as most people were being very cautious. All of a sudden an SUV passed us on the right (remember, in India they drive on the other side of the road, like the British) at a fairly good pace. Within fifteen seconds, we all came to an abrupt halt. In India, when traffic comes to a stop, vehicles start moving from behind and try to slowly pass and jockey for position. In this case, the cars began to choke the road as nothing was moving.

We sat in our vehicle for ten minutes or so. Raja turned off the engine. Then he and Tony decided to go check out what had happened. With the hazard lights flicking a harmonious beat, I could make out their shadowy figures until they were enveloped by the fog. They were gone for about ten minutes. Sadhna and I sat in silence.

Eventually, they came back and said there was a terrible accident just ahead. It turned out the SUV that passed us had collided head-on with a truck and there were two fatalities. The problem was that no traffic was moving in any direction. Everyone had tried to snake along out of their lanes, causing a massive backlog on our side heading to Amritsar, but equally, it meant that no emergency vehicles from Amritsar could make it to the scene because the same situation was happening on the other side. Roadside assistance in this case was people leaving their vehicles and trying to do what they could. No sirens or flashing lights to be seen, no flares or people with reflective vests to keep traffic moving.

We sat for what seemed a very long time. I was thinking about what we had just experienced. Driving in India is dangerous and very risky. I started to feel vulnerable now without seat belts, where before I had been amused by the way cars dashed about.

We were getting tired and hungry. We had been on the road for eight hours already and it was about 7 p.m. Slowly, vehicles started to pull over to the edge of the roadway and we began rolling forward. All the vehicles tried to manoeuvre back to their lane, looking for their place. Tony stuck his head out the window. Raja had to drive gingerly as we moved to the extreme left of the road to get around all the congestion and the accident. There was a ditch to our left and Tony was telling Raja how much room he had before we would roll in, and by Tony's estimation it was about a foot or less as he used his hands to demonstrate the space to Raja. We inched forward, and then we saw the mayhem. A large truck had rolled into the ditch to our right and the entire front end of the SUV that had passed us was crushed in.

As we drove by, the fog remained fairly thick, but you could make out the shadow and outline of two bodies that had been pulled from the wreckage and placed on the side of the road. It was an eerie feeling to know that just a few seconds before the crash happened, that car had whizzed by us. We were grateful to be moving again and leaving this situation. Up to this point, I had been feeling that we had experienced magnificence in some of the things we had seen, like the Taj Mahal, as well as some challenges with our luggage not showing up on time and the Janpath Hotel fiasco. But now, on the road, I was questioning whether we were really ready for India. The locals could deal with this way of life, but the situation made me feel very much a foreigner.

We were still forty kilometres from our destination of Amritsar. We had now been on the road for about ten hours. Fatigue was starting to replace hunger for all of us. With all the fog, it seemed we were driving with very little light or sense of direction. Every second, the orange hazard lights would flash on and off so Tony could maintain his view of the road. At first, I had wondered why Tony was coming along, but now, after this experience, I understood how important it was to have him with us.

Eventually, our pace picked up as we passed the clot of traffic. Buildings and houses came into sight, and more and more lights flickered in the distance as the fog seemed to ease its tight grip on us. We must be nearing Amritsar, as traffic increased. The fog was mixed with dust from passing cars. I could hear the sound of scooters buzzing by and horns everywhere. It was almost 9 p.m., but there were a lot of people walking about. The roadside stalls were in full operation; stores with all their goods were lit up and welcoming. Raja was now on a mission to find our hotel. As in Delhi, he would stop and ask and then we would be off again. Eventually, we arrived at the Ritz Plaza hotel. It was all lit up, with bands playing and beautifully colourful outfits everywhere. It turned out that a wedding was in full force.

The gentleman at the front desk was pleasant and well-dressed, unlike the guy at Janpath. He said he had our reservation but there were no rooms. *What*? "Here we go again!" I said. Turns out that due to the tremendous fog in the area, the airport was closed and flights were cancelled, so people had wound up staying longer. I explained how long we had been travelling and that we were very tired. He understood our plight and said he could put us up at one of their other hotels. We said no, we had booked this hotel and we wanted our room.

By now Sadhna had come up to the desk and learned of the situation, and she started to tell the hotel manager that she was not going anywhere and that they had better come up with a room. I stepped aside at this point, as I knew the volcano was about to explode. The manager said for us to go to the dining room and have dinner and he would sort things out. Sadhna would have none of this and said we would wait there. Eventually, the manager conceded that they had one last room that someone else had reserved, but they had not yet arrived, so he would give us their room and the hotel would have to deal with the consequences when the other unfortunate guests arrived.

With that, we had our key. We let Raja know and he left for the night but said he would be back in the morning. Sadhna and I got to our room and dropped our bags on the floor and crashed on the bed. I don't think I was ever happier to be given access to a room. Even the Janpath Hotel would have been welcoming at that point.

After long, hot showers, we were both ready for dinner about 10 p.m. As we walked into the dining room, we were led to our table and there on a small stage was a sitar and tabla player (two drums side by side). The music was soothing and I felt I could have fallen asleep right there. We got some vegetarian dishes and rotis and called it a night. We were very tired and the bed was a welcome relief.

15

SEEKING
SIKHISM

I WOKE AROUND 5 a.m., and even though it was early, I felt I'd had a good night's sleep. I lay there in a peaceful, quiet space. I was mentally preparing for the day and the visit to the Golden Temple of Amritsar. I was feeling somewhat worn out, because we had spent a week travelling about and experiencing a small section of India—the key word being "experiencing," because I think there were two factors at play.

First, in the past, whenever I went anywhere on vacation, I would just go with the flow and see the sites with a touristy eye. I never really tried to appreciate the place the way the locals viewed it. My previous trips had involved getting on a big bus with other tourists, being driven around, stopping at places for a little while, taking photos, and making it back to the hotel in an easy fashion. Every so often the loudspeaker would come on and announce, "If you look to your left, you will see blah blah blah," but we would just keep driving and I would try to take a quick snapshot as we passed by. It was as simple as watching television, but, like television, it was to be watched rather than experienced. I saw what was intended to be seen and that was all. "Off the beaten track" didn't exist for me.

Second, I think on this trip I was more curious, receptive, and reflective because it was a journey of discovery. I am glad I did not do the trip ten years earlier, because I don't think I would have been ready to experience India in all its glory, with its good and bad sides. I think I had matured as a traveller and was now ready to really *see* and not just observe.

As a British-born Canadian whose Indian identity was intertwined with Fijian roots, I was not sure what my experience in the Punjab would be. Was I Indian, Canadian, or a mix? Physically, it is obvious that I am Indian, but within, who am I? How does my Indian background play with my Canadian sense? Or maybe I was thinking about this all wrong and segmenting myself too much. Lying there staring blankly at the ceiling, I wondered if I am perhaps a blend rather than a composite of many parts.

I found myself thinking about a rice dish my mother used to make when I was growing up. It is called kitchari. Kitchari is a dish you whip up that is convenient and commonplace in Indian cooking; the North American equivalent might be an omelette—quick and easy. You go to your fridge, pull out whatever vegetables you have, add lentils and rice, sprinkle in some spices, and there you have a beautifully blended dish with flavour (and one that is much more glamorous than an omelette!). A realization hit me, and I abruptly sat up. I am kitchari! I am a blend of flavours, and maybe a rather spicy kitchari at that. For the first time, I knew that I had been looking at my life all wrong and that maybe there were parts of me that did fit into this muddled and exotic place. I was starting to feel as though part of me belonged here.

I thought about my name. I was born Ajit, but at a very young age I became Sam. Ajit was always my legal name while Sam was more of an adopted name. I felt shame and regret at having pushed away such a nice name. While growing up, I was embarrassed to be called Ajit, and now, in India, I felt that some might judge me when they saw me as an Indian using the name Sam. They might think that I was Westernized and "too good for us." Even if I wanted to, I could not be known as Ajit now, because my identity had a solid reputation. I was Sam. I accepted this, and also pondered how I might interpret my name going forward. I accepted that "Sam" is used casually, my everyday name, but when "Ajit" is used, it is as if I have put on a nice formal suit. "Ajit" makes a more profound statement.

I knew that this part of the journey was going to be important, because it would strike at my very foundations. I am Sikh, but perhaps in name only, and even then, there is that division between Ajit and Sam.

Sikhism is a part of me, but not to an extent where I feel it is fully embraced. This is not because I reject Sikhism, but rather because I never really learned about it while growing up in Canada. I don't practise the teachings, and my visits to the gurdwara near my home are infrequent. However, when I do step into a gurdwara, I am in a peaceful place. I may not understand the words to the hymns, and I may catch only small bits of the speeches that I can decipher, but I do feel a connection to Sikhism.

It is a fine balance that I live. On the one hand, I find comfort and peace when I am at the gurdwara, sitting there listening to the hymns; however, at the same time, I really don't understand the words or rituals, and just try to mimic the people around me who are far more versed in the ways of Sikhism. Part of me senses a strong connection, but another part of me feels like an observer. This idea of balance can also be applied to any situation where I am in the presence of a faith. Being neutral about religion, I often feel as though I am a bystander to a secret society of believers, and will only appreciate a part of what is shown to me. All of that said, I do wear a universal and visible symbol of Sikhism, the *kara* (a steel or iron bangle). I feel that the *kara* symbolizes my attachment to my background and ancestors; I wear it out of respect for them and because it reminds me of who I am.

Still in bed, thoughts of my identity continued to swirl around in my mind. Part of coming to India and visiting the Golden Temple was about discovering an aspect of my life that I had never really realized. I can speak Hindi conversationally, but understanding Punjabi is far more difficult. When I took a Punjabi class prior to my travels to India, I found that about 80 percent of the words I use in Hindi are very similar to Punjabi, except in Punjabi they speak lightning fast and it is a more abrupt language, so I have a more difficult time connecting words.

I know many Western people with international roots who might relate to my "kitchari" sentiment. One foot is solidly planted in the Western world where you have grown up, but another foot rests on your cultural upbringing, which is ever-present but not necessarily evident. Sometimes it can be an inner struggle, like putting drops of paint into a watercolour piece: it spreads across the surface rather than staying a solid colour, strong and obvious. The watercolours blend with the surface and you are a watered-down version of something else. You try so hard to fit in that you start to replace your foundation with another one. You don't want your friends to see you eating a roti and curry for fear they might think you are not one of them, but at the same time, you like roti and curry because it is comfort food, and also tasty!

Sometimes, when I meet Indo-Canadians, they assume that I am Indian, too, and so they automatically speak Punjabi, or throw Punjabi into the conversation. Even though I try my hardest to understand them, it is like watching a movie with subtitles that go too fast, or as if I'm hard of hearing and pretending to understand what is being said. Sometimes you just nod and smile and hope you are not agreeing to an arranged marriage. Other times, Canadians will ask me what part of India I am from—not in a bad way, but more inquisitively. When I respond, they are quite surprised, because they had assumed I grew up there. So I suppose it is easy to make assumptions and assessments rather than asking a question and listening.

I admit that I carried a sense of loss prior to visiting India—because I had an idea of who I was but it did not really fit the picture that others held. To some extent my journey was about proving to myself and others that I am Indian, and worthy of that title.

For me, visiting the Golden Temple and seeking out my roots felt like trying to renovate the unfinished basement of a house. The frame was there, but not the completed walls. I was not feeling whole. I was not sure how prepared I was. What does it mean to be Sikh? What would I encounter at the Golden Temple? Would it be like attending a temple in Vancouver, or visiting a significant site so I could cross it off my list, or would it prove to be something more deep and meaningful?

To put things into context, it may be helpful to talk a little about Sikhism—to help establish what I grew up understanding and how it was a part of my upbringing. Of course, Hinduism was also part of my personal mosaic. Sikhism is who I am by birth, but Hinduism was introduced to me by family because of our ties to the Fijian community.

Growing up around the faith, I developed an understanding of it but without the depth or feeling of

A *kara* (steel bangle) and *kirpan* (small dagger) symbolize the need to defend and help those who can not help themselves.

significance that a traditional Sikh household would have imparted. We did not have a prayer room or time allocated to understanding Sikhism. So as a young person, I looked to fill in the missing pieces. For example, I never wore a turban, except when I married. I was amazed that the head covering comprises six yards of material, and for those who know how to tie it, it is not a difficult task. If I were to tie a turban today, it would be a clumpy ball of material on my head and I would be doing an injustice to the faith. The turban, tied properly and with pleats, looks very distinguished. But why do Sikhs wear a turban? What is the significance? Simple questions, but I had to discover the answers myself.

I could easily google Sikhism, and copy and paste a lesson so that you might be better informed, but I feel it is more important to provide my own perspective so you can appreciate my view. Think of it as Sikhism through the eyes of a modern-day kitchari soul.

My understanding of Sikhism is that it is a relatively new religion (only about 600 years old) within the spectrum of ideologies that have embraced the doctrines of respect and honour. If world religions, such as Hinduism, Islam, Judaism, Buddhism, and Christianity were founded 1,500 or 2,000 years ago, or even longer ago than that, are their practices and ideologies still relevant to the modern world? This is not to question how valid these religions are, but rather to point out that they have gone through some alterations over time while retaining their foundational aspects. I'm not suggesting that Sikhism is right and the other religions are wrong, but rather that Sikhism tried to incorporate a number of ideologies that already existed.

Perched between Islam and Hinduism, did Sikhism blend the two to create its doctrines, or did it form organically? Or could it be both—that it witnessed both faiths and created something new from them? My appreciation is only at the surface level and I am not qualified to speak to Sikhism's origins. I can only imagine how challenging it must have been to talk about a new ideology that paled in comparison with the two giants of Hinduism and Islam. I equate it to growing up in a strict household with the parents setting the rules and a child deciding to go in their own direction. The upheaval must have been a huge struggle.

While Muslims have the Quran, Hindus the Gita, and Christians the Bible, Sikhs have the Granth Sahib. It is the teachings of the ten gurus who established the foundations of Sikhism. They are not considered gods, but rather spiritual voices and beings who put here to enlighten us. When one is in the presence of the Granth, you must have your head covered to show respect. It could be a turban or a head scarf called a *rumāl*.

What I truly value about Sikhism are the doctrines. Fortunately, these were inculcated in me before I started to understand the faith. The religion has a few key elements that really appealed to me, but these doctrines are also important principles in most world religions:

- **Work ethic:** One of the foundations is the idea that no matter how difficult the struggle or whatever needs to be done, you should always aim for the highest quality and never shy away from challenges. Hard work will result in a strong character, which will form a more solid individual.

- *Sewa*: This word means giving back to help those less fortunate. No matter a person's situation, you cannot turn your back on them and must always lend a helping hand. We need to step up and be contributors rather than bystanders.

- **Defender**: Related to *sewa*, this doctrine says you should always defend those who cannot defend themselves, regardless of faith. Stand up and support those who are oppressed.

- **Respect towards others**: Sikhism recognized that the world was already made up of key religions and that there are always clashes between groups who claim they are right and the rest of the world is wrong. Sikhs believe that the world can be made up of different faiths, which must all be respected. If you are going to practise Hinduism, be the best Hindu possible. To be Muslim, you must be the best Muslim you can be.

Sikhs are easy to spot. They wear five identifiable symbols of their faith. We call these the Five Ks, and they mark one as orthodox and a follower of Sikhism. I hold on to only one of the Five Ks, that being the steel bangle, or *kara*. The Five Ks are:

- *Kara*: A steel or iron bangle worn on the wrist. It is a simple symbol: one solid, round piece of metal. There is no beginning and no end, but rather one constant. The *kara* represents life and is worn at all times as a constant reminder of the faith. You could say it's similar to a Christian's crucifix.

- *Kesh*: Sikhs, from the time they are born, never cut their hair. This long hair is called the *kesh*, and it is a sign that you appreciate what you were born with; you are not to alter your appearance as God created it. Also, the *kesh* makes a Sikh easily identifiable. It is associated with the turban, which Sikhs wear to keep the *kesh* tidy and respectable.

- *Kangha* or *kanga*: Related to the *kesh* is the *kangha*. The *kangha* is a small wooden comb that is tucked away in the hair under a turban and symbolizes cleanliness and the importance of always keeping one's appearance respectable.

- *Kacchera* or *kachera*: An undergarment which symbolizes that one is ready for whatever one has to face and reminds the wearer of purity, as it covers the lower extremities. The *kacchera* looks like boxer shorts with a drawstring.

- *Kirpan*: A small dagger worn to the side, which signifies the defending of truth. It is also a sign of defending those who are not able to defend themselves. It is not to be used unless the situation is grave and it is required.

Sikhs believe in an egalitarian society; men and women are equal in the eyes of God. This is why Sikh names can be unisex. For example, my name is Ajit, but Ajit can be a male or a female name, and the way to differentiate is by the middle name. "Singh" denotes a male and signifies a lion, while a female's middle name is "Kaur," which symbolizes a princess. So if you are ever in a situation where you have a Sikh name and you are not sure if the person is male or female, consider the middle name and it should become obvious. Ajit Singh Thiara is a male while Ajit Kaur Thiara would be a female.

Going to the Golden Temple would enable me to bring together my upbringing and my understanding. I decided it was time to rise and take a long shower— a cleansing of sorts, as I would be visiting the holiest place for Sikhs. People go to Amritsar to experience the Golden Temple for religious reasons; for me, it was more a pilgrimage to discover myself.

16

FEELING GOOD AS GOLD

The Golden Temple

A S I TOWELLED myself off, I reflected on what was going to be a pivotal point in my trip. I had one week under my belt, had not got sick, and was orienting to the life before me. Even though the more than ten hours of travel the day before had been tiring, I had refused to put on headphones and sleep through the journey. If I had, I would have missed so much of my trip. I told myself, *Okay, this week is my trip in the Punjab, and it is going to be very important.* I would keep my eyes open. The search for my roots was going to be either euphoric or a total letdown. Would people say, "I told you so!" and "You wasted your time chasing something that you had very little hope of accomplishing"? I tried to concentrate on the spiritual importance of where I was and what I might experience at the Golden Temple. I needed as much spiritual intervention as possible.

I pulled out a maroon Indian tunic that I had purchased in Agra, and a maroon *rumāl* because you must have your head covered when entering any Sikh temple. Sadhna wore a simple beige-and-burgundy Indian suit with a burgundy dupatta (a woman's long piece of material to cover the head).

I wanted to keep breakfast simple and vegetarian. It did not seem right to have any meat or eggs when I would be in a holy place, so I had aloo (potato) curry, roti, and dahi (plain yogurt). My stomach was full and now I needed to feed my soul.

About 8:30 a.m., Raja showed up. He said he would be showing us around today and that Tony would join us tomorrow. The air was cool and there was still a thick layer of fog, though nothing like the day before. As I walked towards the four-by-four, I was wondering if it was actually fog or smoke from people burning wood or cow patties as fuel for cooking.

Raja said that we were not far from the Harimandir Sahib, more commonly known as the Golden Temple. He said he would be nearby once we got there, but he wanted us to really appreciate the place and not just see it as tourists. "Explore it on your own and make this your journey," he said. He would tell us the history and details later if we needed them. I was pleased to hear this, as it would allow me the space to really experience the Golden Temple.

As we drove around, we saw city walls made of bricks and mortar that had aged with the times and the busy life of Amritsar. The city was bustling, with dust kicked up by the moving traffic and people. Roadside dentists, barbers, and food stalls, and pretty much anything you needed, were within arm's length. I was amazed by the ingenuity of the small roadside businesses. Contraptions had been assembled from discarded metals and rubber to form the places of business and, at times, the required tools or the merchandise, which functioned to solve any individual's problems. Your trousers needed hemming? Not a problem. Two stalls down was a quick repair place with a lone person, a stool, and a mending box at the ready.

Whereas I had rarely seen turbans in Delhi, Agra, or Jaipur, here there was an abundance of them. People were walking about doing their daily business wearing their head scarves and neatly tied turbans. The women wore shalwar kameez, Indian suits comprising a long tunic, baggy pants, and a loosely wrapped head scarf. While in Rajasthan people wore bright colours, in the Punjab the colours were subtler. We passed street stalls where early risers were having breakfast. I saw the *chaiwalla* pouring tea with ease from one glass cup to another in front of a crowd awaiting the frothy mix to start their day. Cars, scooters, tuk-tuks, and bikes meandered through the alleyways. Rickshaws with kids neatly dressed in uniforms headed to school in a convoy. I felt a great sense of anticipation as we neared our destination.

A short while later, our vehicle came to a stop and Raja informed us that we had arrived. We got out and looked around. I felt a crispness in the air and could see my breath. The Punjab sits farther north in India and we were visiting in winter. While the Golden Temple wasn't visible, we could see all the people going in the same direction and knew this was the place to be.

I pulled on the *rumāl* and Sadhna adjusted her dupatta over her head. As we walked up to the entrance, there were sinks to our right and left and a moat right in front of us. Behind us was a bunker-style structure that was mostly below the surface but had large windows just above ground. There were people inside and we had to remove our shoes, bend down, and hand them to an attendant through the open window. He gave us a numbered ticket so we could retrieve them later. This was different from Hindu temples we had visited, where your shoes sat in a pile unattended and there was a risk of someone taking them.

I realized that the reason for the sinks and moat was so that you could wash your hands and face, as well as your feet, before entering this holy place. A cleansing of sorts. The running water in the sinks was cold. I rinsed my hands and face thoroughly and proceeded to walk through the moat, which was about five feet wide and two inches deep. The water was quite cold, but there were only a few steps to take. There was no way to reach the stairs that led to the temple without going through the moat. Someone had designed this very well.

Our hands, faces, and feet were clean, so we could now proceed to the temple. We slowly walked up the marble stairs and finally caught a glimpse of the top of the Golden Temple. Each step revealed more magnificence. Finally, at the top of the stairs, I stood in awe and silently took in the view.

In the middle of a large artificial lake was the Harimandir Sahib, the Golden Temple. Around the lake was a symmetrical marble walkway with archways and religious buildings, which created almost a city wall. I was so caught up in the beauty of the Golden Temple that I was no longer aware of any of the distractions outside the wall. It felt as though the buildings were a barrier and the sounds outside had dissipated, replaced by the soothing *kirtans* (hymns), and so we were standing in a peaceful oasis. The fog lightly shrouded the temple, which stood prominently with its bright gold roof. It resembled an artwork more than anything else, as if the artist had painted the images with a hazy tone. The sounds of instruments being played and hymns being sung penetrated the fog with a soft, rhythmic tone that added to the glow of the temple roof.

I closed my eyes, felt the familiar coolness of the marble beneath my feet, and drew my hands together. I stood there for a while taking in the sounds and eventually opened my eyes. I looked around and saw a few pilgrims seated on the marble floor facing the Golden Temple, each one in their own spiritual world. Who were they? Where did they come from? What were their joys and pleasures, challenges and obstacles? They sat close together but also separate, sending a message that they needed spiritual space but required others' presence at the same time.

TOP Sadhna and I soaking in the spirituality of the Golden Temple.

BOTTOM Shrouded in fog and hymns, the Golden Temple at Amritsar was mystical.

There were turbaned men and men in *rumāls*, women with their shalwar kameez and dupattas, and kids with their hair in buns and holding on to the hands of their parents. Everyone had their own purpose for being here.

A few of the men standing around wore coloured robes and large turbans, and carried spears. The colours were striking and distinct: blues, yellows. These were the guards of the temple and they stood their sentry duty with purpose and conviction. They had adopted a life of service to protect the temple. They stood tall with long, flowing beards. There were no ranks or medals here, just honour.

I wondered if anyone from my village had ever been here. Had my grandfather visited as a youth? Or was I the first in my family to stand on this holy ground? I tried to be very present and slow my mind from wandering. It was as if I was trying ice cream for the first time, and I wanted to taste the flavour and use all of my senses to best appreciate what I had just discovered. I had seen photos of the Golden Temple and watched a few documentaries, but until you are there, you will not have true appreciation. I was standing in front of brilliance.

After a long while, I broke my concentration and began to move my thoughts more to "what" I was experiencing over "why" I was there. I walked to the edge of the lake and saw stairs that led down to the water. To the side was a tall, slim pilgrim dressed in a turban and a *kacchera* (one of the Five Ks, the undergarment). He was holding a chain that connected him to the top of the stairs and immersing himself in the cold water. He was cleansing his soul, standing there with his hands drawn in prayer towards the Golden Temple and his eyes closed. The devotion of this person, who did not fear the cold water, was striking. As he entered it, a ripple shook the stillness of the lake and the reflection of the Golden Temple began to dance.

I realized that the experience was going to be different for me than for Sadhna. As a Hindu, she was there to experience the site and gain a cultural understanding over any spiritual outcomes. We all have our own reasons for being present, and I knew this was something special for me and not just a place to visit. My soul was hungry for what I would encounter.

I took a seat on the cold marble floor like the pilgrims and crossed my legs. It was not the most comfortable position, but slowly the slight pain dissipated and I got comfortable and took some deep breaths. I was about four feet from the water's edge, and I once again closed my eyes to appreciate what was being given to me at this point, a glimpse of my identity. For once in India, I felt I belonged. Not like the devout seeker in the water, but rather as someone seeking within himself. This was a place to contemplate self and life. I was trying to harness stillness. Part of me knew that this was a place to be experienced, and I wanted to explore as much as possible, like a kid in an amusement park. But another part wanted to just stop and savour the moment, to slow down and be present. It took a bit of doing, but I was able to slow down, take some deep breaths, and calm my mind. I think the hymns helped me to concentrate because I focused on what I heard, and it was hypnotic.

Eventually, I opened my eyes. I now felt like exploring this place. We got up and started to walk again, but we took our time. I wanted every step to have purpose. This was not your typical "walk around, take some pictures, and keep walking" kind of place. Strolling along the water, I saw massive koi in the lake. They were fattened up by the prasad (sweets made of flower, ghee, and sugar) offered in the temple. Eventually, we stood on the footbridge that led to the centre of the lake. I observed young, old, male, and female on this pilgrimage. They were entering a place that would feed and cleanse their soul. Would it do the same for me?

The Harimandir Sahib had a magnificent soft gold glow. It did not seem all that big compared with the overall grounds and lake, but it certainly had a presence. The white marble walls glistened and the gold inverted lotus flower roof gleamed. The hymns continued to ring out from the loudspeakers, and the sound was mesmerizing and soothing to the heart and soul. Instinct told me to clasp my hands together.

I walked softly along the footbridge, appreciating the structure. It seemed that the only way to approach this holy place was along this narrow passage over the lake. The people in front of us and behind us were all silent. They came from all faiths; all that mattered was that they were there for an enlightening experience. I think many of the Sikhs in line sought out the journey because of their devotion; going to the temple reaffirmed their faith in Sikhism. I knew I was there to find myself, that I was no longer a tourist but a pilgrim.

The great hall was brightly lit and filled with people. The Granth (holy book) was before us in the centre of the room. Perched next to it was a bearded Sikh gentleman who read verse after verse into a microphone. The words rang out, and while I did not understand them, they struck a chord. I found a place to the side and behind the Granth, and we both sat cross-legged by the barrier. I was about ten feet away from the centre and the holy book. After a few more verses, the *kirtans* (hymns) started. I sat there listening and absorbing everything. While the room was crowded, it felt empty— as if nothing existed at that moment except me and the Granth. I felt a sense of euphoria and calmness, and relief at having arrived.

I closed my eyes and the *kirtans* penetrated me. I began thinking of my family and friends, my experiences, my journey to India, and what the future might hold. I was trying to embrace a blessing for the entire world: for hardships to be removed, pain to be gone, hate to disappear. I was praying for the world—and I don't pray! It was as if someone had put a blanket around me to comfort me, and I began to weep—not in sadness, but because I felt overwhelmed. A weeping that was deep within me, from a place that I never knew existed. With my eyes closed, the tears streamed down my face and I could feel the droplets scaling down and falling to my clasped hands at chest level. Were the tears a sign of pain leaving my body? Were they my way of appreciating something that I never really embraced? All I know is that I felt a calmness that I had never felt before. It just felt right.

I opened my eyes and pulled out the small photograph of the village, and through the blurriness of my tears I gently held it between my fingers. I needed strength at this point. Something was telling me that my quest to find my roots was a noble cause and that I would be offered the spiritual support I needed. I knew that my journey to find my village—whether I found it or not—was going to provide something for my soul. If I was not successful, I would experience life lessons and would refuse to see this as a setback. I was now ready for the final push to find the people we had lost years ago.

Putting the photo away, I got up and gingerly walked between people so as not to disturb them. We meandered into another room. I felt a sense of purpose like I had never felt before. Raja appeared before us, as he had stealthily been following us around while always remaining in the background. He wanted to show us a few rooms and places before we left. He made sure to take us to a room where one of the oldest versions of the Granth was placed. There, the book was being read as well, and we were told that there are shifts so the book is read 24-7 without a break. A chain of faith has been created over the years, and the devotees are there to keep the chain alive.

We bid farewell to the centre building and walked back outside into the foggy morning and along the other side of the footbridge. All who entered exited the same way. I stood there to collect my thoughts. I had changed. Not in a religious sense but a spiritual one. I felt a connection to this place and the forces around it. I had walked in with burdens and walked out cleansed and purified. Slowly, we walked along the footbridge and around the square, listening to the hymns and looking at the Harimandir from many vantage points. We were provided offerings of prasad, and consumed them. I also received some offerings of large sugar granules, almonds, and something that was white, sweet, and crunchy that I wanted to take home to the family.

Slowly strolling about, we came to the Sikh museum. Raja wanted us to see some of the historical aspects of the Golden Temple. I have to admit that after the spiritual cleanse, I really did not want to learn the historical aspects of Sikhism by reading labels in a museum. It would have been nicer to have visited this place before experiencing the Golden Temple. However, I did walk about and looked at different artifacts and paintings, and learned more about Sikhism.

As I toured the museum, I saw an elderly gentleman with a regal look about him. He stood tall in a long black tunic, with a long grey beard and a neatly tied black turban. He held himself with dignity, and greeted us. His eyes crinkled when he smiled, and there was a warmth about him as he embraced my hands and welcomed us in English. When I told him about this being our first visit to India, the search for my roots and identity, he was moved. We spoke for a while and appreciated being in each other's company. As we parted, he again grasped my hands and then touched my forehead and wished me well on my adventure. His genuineness was the real gift the museum held for me. The artifacts and paintings were somewhat interesting, but his kindness was the Sikhism that I have come to know.

This day renewed my appreciation for the Sikh faith and gave me more understanding of my background and where I come from in a spiritual sense. It offered me a glimpse of my ancestors and what they followed and believed. It provided more of an anchor on who I am and a bit of a spiritual road map to where I'm from and where I might go. I have been fortunate to travel to many spiritual places: church, temple, beach, mountain, forest. Each has a feeling of a unifying force to which one can open your mind and heart. Though I am Sikh, I choose not to be limited to one faith. I would rather travel and explore various cultures and religions with an open mind and see how people embrace their calling. This visit to Amritsar told me to continue to be a good person and help others. That is all that the Sikh faith has asked of me: to carry our doctrine of *sewa* (supporting others) and to continue along the path of hard work in order to help others on their journey.

Raja, Sadhna, and I walked along in silence, with me lagging behind. I turned around at the top of the entrance stairs and faced the Harimandir one last time. My time here felt too short; there was so much more for me to experience, to explore, to understand. I closed my eyes, bowed down, and touched the marble floor with my fingers, bringing them to my forehead and then my heart. I opened my eyes, and with a few remaining tears I said goodbye to a very important place in my life.

I turned and walked down the stairs, the Golden Temple inched out of my sight, and the *kirtans* faded into the background, still audible but no longer pronounced. I left with an internal light brighter than when I came in.

17

LESSONS
IN HISTORY

---

*Jallianwala Bagh |
Wagah Border*

WALKING OUT OF the cloak of comfort and silence, we were now confronted with a bustling city. It was as if I had emerged from a protective force field or was abruptly waken from a restful sleep. The calmness of the Harimandir was behind us, replaced by the honking of car horns and people all around us. In the open-air market, I found a few things that I might like to hold as mementoes of my experience. I bought a blue *rumāl* for future visits to Sikh temples, a *kirpan* (the small ceremonial dagger) that is a physical reminder of the Golden Temple, and a *kara* (steel bracelet). Simple items, but they held significance and meaning. Over the noise of the streets, I could faintly hear the hymns and songs in the distance until they faded out.

Raja, Sadhna, and I strolled a short distance between crowded streets and buildings. The signs that surrounded us were weathered, written in Hindi only or a mix of Hindi and English. I was trying to decipher some of the signs, which were poorly written. I was bemused as a person walked past us selling fake beards. Not sure why anyone would need a fake beard in a part of the world where most of the men already have beards, but it was their livelihood.

It was now about 1 p.m. and we were quite hungry. We found a small place at the bottom of one of these buildings to have lunch. It was open to the air and not the cleanest spot, but it looked inviting. We ordered a type of roti, a curry dish, and chai. The chai arrived first, and the steam from the hot drink rose into the cool air in a casual swirl. The drink was sweet and thick, and it warmed me. After a few chais and a hearty lunch, we were ready to venture out again. My soul and stomach were both full now.

Raja wanted to show us a part of Amritsar that I had heard of and seen in the movie *Gandhi*. Jallianwala Bagh was historically significant because of the massacre that occurred there on April 13, 1919, during the time of the British Raj and the struggle for independence. At that period, there were a lot of political tensions between Brits and Indians. Public gatherings were not permitted, but in Jallianwala Bagh, about 10,000 people arrived for a political rally. The British, upon hearing this, dispatched troops under the command of General Reginald Dyer. He issued the order to fire upon the crowd, and with the only exit from the park blocked by the troops, about 1,000 people lost their lives that day. It became a tragic turning point that eventually led to the end of British colonial rule in India.

Now, the site is a lovely garden. Walking through a narrow corridor leading to the gardens, I tried to imagine the brutal history of this place. A small part of me realized that the country of my birth and the country of my ancestral roots were intertwined and conflicted, and together they polarized this country into the masses who were oppressed and seeking their independence and the minority who attempted to hold back the tide and protect the status quo in their own self-interest.

Those there today, were they aware of the history? There were people wandering around, taking pictures of themselves in front of the flora, talking and laughing and sitting on benches. I stopped to stare at a young man lying on a bench, looking up to the trees and chatting on his phone. This was the modern India that had moved forward from a troubled past.

I walked up to a brick wall that was exposed behind some shrubs and ran my fingers along the surface. The wall was old and I noted an indentation about an inch in diameter. Was this just an effect of weathering, or could it be a bullet hole?

Raja informed us that we had one more stop to make today: Wagah Border. He explained to us, as we were driving, that Wagah Border is the entry point to Pakistan. It is a fortified border, an official place to cross from one country to the other. We parked our vehicle and strolled to the area. We walked up to the gate and there were bleachers on both sides, like you would see in a high school stadium. Raja explained to us that later in the day, when the border closed, there would be pomp and ceremony. It is a party atmosphere with music, dancing, and people milling around, and at a certain point the border closes and the military comes in. People cheer and whistle in the stands. We were not able to stay for the ceremony, but if I ever return, this is something I would like to experience.

Using exaggerated hand gestures, Raja explained that there is a large swing gate and this is where the boundary between Pakistan and India sits. We listened intently as he described the situation, with soldiers parading about in large plume turbans and goose steps. Every move is exaggerated to impress the audience. Soldiers stare each other down, but at the same time it is ceremonial and I am sure they must be winking or smiling a bit. Flags are simultaneously lowered. The two sides mirror each other, the Indian side in khaki-coloured uniforms and the Pakistanis in black. Both sides march in parallel while mirroring their moves, and in the end two officers make their way to the centre and on the borderline march towards each other, give a ceremonial handshake and salute, turn around, and walk back to their respective sides, while the other soldiers slam the gate behind them to close the border.

This show is a theatrical playing out of the real tensions that have existed between these two countries since partition in 1947, when people were displaced

I was captivated by this beautiful stone statue of the Hindu god Shiva.

from their homes and the Muslims made their way to Pakistan, and the Hindus and Sikhs to India. Partition was an ugly divorce that created the two countries as we know them today. Thousands of people were murdered and property was pillaged as mobs attacked each other. Over the years, the strains in the Indian-Pakistani relationship have reached flashpoints at different times, and currently tensions are simmering. The main source of conflict at the moment is Kashmir, a disputed border region between the two countries.

As we drove back to the hotel, we passed open fields and sparsely populated areas, and I felt I could have been in Canada. I was quiet on the ride back, as I reflected on the beauty of my experience at the Golden Temple. The trip thus far had been hectic and full, as I tried to grasp what India had to offer me. I closed my eyes and attempted to blend the various elements that constituted India for me: the sound of the *kirtans*, the calm and the busyness, the serenity and the hastiness of life. India can be everything! You can find quiet, harmonious places amidst the noise and rush.

More and more, India began to reflect my own life. India represented something that had always been part of me: the four elements of water, air, fire, and earth. In me, there is a calmness (water), I live a busy life full of activities (air), I'm passionate (fire), and I try to stay grounded in the present (earth). To me, the four elements had been represented in my experiences in India to date, as I encountered the daily life of the people, the calmness one can feel, the contentment and happiness with little. India is about appreciating life for what it can offer you.

My thoughts on India and my life were taking me deeper and deeper into my personal feelings and helping me better appreciate and understand who I am. Suddenly, I was brought back to reality when Raja said: "Okay, we are not far from your hotel now. Tomorrow I will be here about 9 a.m. and we can get you checked out, and then we begin the search for your *pind*."

Abruptly, it dawned on me that I was entering a very important part of my journey. I had started to find myself, but now it was time to find my ancestral roots. One can venture out on a journey and then take side paths. The universe had already provided me the opportunity to find the part of myself that was lost, by visiting the Golden Temple and seeing other sights and sounds of India. Was that really the hidden gem of this trip, and what I had been seeking all along? Maybe the reason for this trip was that I had been lost, and perhaps the village would remain lost. Questions were racing through my mind. If I didn't find the *pind*, could I be satisfied that at least I had been able to capture my own identity? Would that be enough? I was in search of something very important, but I had uncovered something of equal significance. I was lost and now I was found.

We reached the hotel as the sun was setting. There was an orange glow all about, but it no longer startled me. The hotel had attractive grounds with bright, colourful lights and music blaring; it was like a typical Bollywood musical inviting us in. Beautifully dressed women and men were entering and leaving the park. As it happened, we were present at a traditional Indian wedding, the second we had encountered at one of our hotels. The celebrations were in full swing and cameras were snapping all the memories. We stood there for a few minutes, soaking it all in. I smiled and told myself to savour the moment. A lot of what happened tomorrow would be beyond my control. I could only try my best and be comfortable with the results.

Some guests came through the magnificent archway leading to the park, two women in very colourful saris and a gentleman in a long Indian tunic. They seemed to be key family members of the wedding party. They could sense we were not from around here. They asked where we were visiting from and when we told them, they said, "Oh, we have some family in Toronto, are you from Toronto?" We told them we were from Vancouver and they said, "That is fine," and then they invited us to join us the celebration. "We realize that you might not know anyone, but that does not mean you can't be part of our family." What a fitting statement. Here I was about to embark on a journey to find my lost family, and someone random wanted me to be a part of theirs.

Normally, I would take advantage of such an opportunity, but my mind was heavy with what we had encountered earlier as well as the daunting task before us. I glanced at Sadhna and with my hands together and drawn up to my chest, I did as the locals do and graciously said, "No, thank you. That is most kind and generous, but it has been a very long day and we have an early start tomorrow. Please share with the bride and groom that we wish them a very happy life together." They replied with their hands drawn to their chests, wonderful smiles, and head bobs, and wished us a pleasant trip.

Before going to bed, I pulled out my bigger map and looked at it one more time. We had only two days to accomplish this. There would be no sightseeing on this part of the journey. I would have to up my game and concentrate on the task at hand. We had a map to take us as far as Jandoli, but what would we do then? How would we find the house, with only an old photograph to guide us?

18

SEARCHING FOR THE HAYSTACK

Amritsar to Jalandhar

I HAD A RESTLESS sleep, the kind a kid has the night before Christmas. We were about to embark on the search for my village. Narrowing down where this village might be was going to be a challenge, and we were not sure exactly where it would lead us. My watch slowly ticked away, and it even looked sometimes as though the hands were going backwards. I waited it out and let my mind wander and wonder. At 5 a.m., I put the kettle on and went back to the map. I was looking at our drive from Amritsar to Jalandhar. I had learned that while it may not seem far on a map, the driving always takes longer than anticipated. I would have to be patient. As dawn set in, we had our breakfast and packed our bags. We checked out, and Raja was waiting for us with

Tony. The morning was crisp but clear, with thankfully no fog. The sounds of the early morning birds and the slight heat from the sun felt comforting. We got into the SUV and the road lay before us.

The drive was fairly uneventful, or perhaps my mind was on the task ahead of me. Either way, random occurrences still resonate with me. A minivan was travelling alongside for a short distance and kept signalling us. Raja just continued driving, but every so often I would look to our left and see about five Hindu priests dressed in orange in the van, frantically waving for us to pull over. They all had long, flowing black hair and beards. I asked Raja why they were waving at us and he said, with a grin, that they had drawn up alongside us a while back and were asking us to pull over because they could see we were tourists and they wanted to do a roadside *puja* (religious service). They would do a superficial prayer, recite a few verses from the Gita (holy book), throw a few grains of rice and flowers at us to shower us with blessings, put a red dot on our forehead, and then ask for a donation or let us know what the donation should be. It was a transactional religious service of sorts.

I smiled, thinking that if they were any more aggressive, they would have tried to run us off the road for religious purposes. I felt like an antelope in the grasslands trying to escape a pack of jackals. At that point, Raja hit the accelerator and they got the hint and pulled over to do a U-turn. I heard David Attenborough's documentary voice in my head, saying in a regal British accent: "The prey, managing to allude their predators,

This was taken somewhere en route to Jandoli. The countryside was a welcome break from the busyness of our trip, and gave us some much needed space to reflect on our travels.

live for another day. The jackals retreat and look for their next victim."

I had heard about the aggressive nature of certain Hindu priests. I am sure there are legitimate ones, but these ones give a bad name to the religion. Anyone who puts the rupee or dollar ahead of the person's blessing is not doing the right thing in life. I appreciate that we come from a privileged society and life, and they are just trying to make a living; it is only when they are persistent or pestering that it becomes unacceptable.

A little farther down the road, I saw these hut-like structures made of wood and straw. They seemed to be dotted around the countryside. I asked Raja what they were and he explained that for some they were houses and for others they were storehouses. We pulled over and saw one nearby. As we walked up to it, I saw that it had these small circular discs stored inside. I was not sure what to make of it, but then it became evident that these were dried cow dung patties, used for outdoor fires. I was intrigued by these compact fire cakes. The dung was mostly grass and, dried out and condensed, it would retain the heat and keep a fire going. Nearby was a lady cooking at an outdoor fire. She had this simple beauty about her, wearing a pink sari and going about her duties. She looked over at us and, giving a casual smile, adjusted the shawl part to cover most of her face and went about her work. Sure enough, right beside her were some of these dung cakes. Raja grabbed one from the hut and said I should take a smell. Reluctantly, I did so, but there was none of the cow poop stink I had imagined, but more of an earthy scent. I was amazed at how resourceful people can be.

We pulled into a *dhaba* in the town of Dhilwan for a break and enjoyed a hot glass of chai and some pakoras and samosas. Sitting outside on cheap plastic chairs around a wobbly plastic table, we savoured the treats and talked about the road ahead. Raja said we were probably an hour away and would check in to the hotel. I had my map with me, and we moved a lot of the items off the table in order to study it with military precision.

We knew where Jalandhar was, we knew where Garhshankar was, and Jandoli was in the same area, about eight kilometres from Garhshankar. Sipping tea, we built our battle plans. Raja said that he had asked around and, from his understanding, we would head southeast from Jalandhar—he moved his finger along the map—through Phagwara and Banga. When we got to Garhshankar, we would catch highway 103A north and pass a number of villages. At Handowal Kalan, we would head east to Jandoli. With that, he circled the area with his finger and tapped the map. This was our mission!

I noted that Jandoli was not on the map, and neither were many of the places he had mentioned, but he had spoken with such authority that I felt confident to some extent, and I was also aware that he always had to ask for directions wherever we travelled. The circle he had made had a larger-than-anticipated radius, more than the ten kilometres we were considering based on the information we had, but I had to trust him as he was the local.

We checked in at the hotel and agreed to reconvene at 2 p.m. to undertake the start of the mission. I wrote in my journal, "I will try our best to find it. Not sure of the welcome or if we will even find it. I sit with anticipation."

19

WHAT IS LOST MIGHT BE FOUND

Jandoli

WE WERE READY. I dressed in an Indian kurta and Sadhna wore a cream-coloured Indian suit. We wanted to look respectable in the eyes of the villagers so that it was not such a shock, and also, after visiting Amritsar and the Golden Temple, it felt right to dress in simple clothes. My happiness intertwined with nervousness at the prospect of possibly finding the village and my grandfather's house. Imagine someone coming to your house unannounced, showing you a picture, and saying that you might be related to them. As I looked in the mirror in the hotel room, I was thinking of every scenario and how to introduce myself. Sort of like going on a first date or meeting the parents for the first time. Standing there,

I was practising my "Hello, how are you, I am a long-lost link to the family." "Hi there, my name is Ajit Thiara, I have come from a long way away to look for you." "Hi there, are you related to me?" Finally, I resolved that I would decide on my words on the spot, if I actually found the village.

Raja opened the door to his truck and said he had asked around and had a very good feeling about Jandoli and today. Before we left, I opened my travel journal and made sure I had the photo carefully placed in there. It was my only connection to the village. We left, and shortly after, we stopped at an Indian sweet shop to pick up some treats for the people in the village. You can never go empty-handed to a family's house. The road to Garhshankar was fairly uneventful—no fog, no vans trying to pull us over, or other distractions—and we made it in good time. From there, as was common by now, Raja pulled over and asked around a bit and was given the directions to Jandoli. With confidence, he pointed forward and we were off.

As we drove, anticipation started to build. I was feeling good. I had done as much as I could to prepare, and now I was taking the test. I looked at the precious photo one more time. Would this even matter, and could I fill in the pieces to explain myself?

We made it to Handowal Kalan, and turned off the highway to Jandoli. As we got closer, we could see more houses. Was one of them the place where my grandfather had embarked on his journey? My heart started to beat faster. As we entered the village, we drove along some side roads and came upon a house. There were people sitting in a dusty, high-walled courtyard, and you could tell it was a family gathering place, their area to relax and share in each other's company. As people walked by, they could stop for a visit. Had my grandfather stopped here?

Looking out of our vehicle, I was careening to see them and they were careening to look back. Raja walked out first and approached them. I could hear him explaining to them who we were and our purpose. I saw some heads nodding and more careening looks and then a wave to say, "Come out, come here." With a smile, we did that. We approached, and it was an extended family sitting outside and enjoying a refreshing cup of chai in the early afternoon sun. Were they part of our family? We went to sit down with them on a dusty bench, but they quickly rushed into the house and came out with chairs so we would be more comfortable. With smiles, they offered us a cup of chai, which we graciously accepted.

As I slowly sipped, I noticed that they had small, simple glasses of tea, while they had given us proper cups. They saw us as guests and not as family, or perhaps as foreigners who might not appreciate the local ways. So even though I was starting to feel more local, the perception was that I was still a foreigner. In Sadhna's fluent Hindi and my fusion of Hindi, Punjabi, and English, we began to communicate. Sadhna spoke with elegance, but my speech was always met with smiles and snickers. We exchanged pleasantries and I handed them a box of the sweets. They opened it, smiled, and then turned

The residents of Jandoli village were so warm and welcoming. They truly wanted to help us find my family's village, but were not able to offer any information that we didn't already have.

the open box to me and asked me to take the first piece. I accepted.

We sat and talked for a while, and during that time they summoned the senior overseer for the village, someone who might be able to offer some guidance and direction. He was a distinguished-looking man in a blue suit and a nicely pleated turban. I assumed he was the village elder. He sat down with us and they brought him a chai as well, in a glass cup, and a refill of chai for us in our china cups. He spoke English and seemed proud to be able to use it. I shared my journey with him, in some Hindi and a lot of English, while Sadhna enjoyed conversing in Hindi. He nodded and smiled as we spoke.

I opened my journal and pulled out the photograph and handed it to him. With a discerning eye, he examined it closely. A smile appeared on his face. "I am not 100 percent sure," he said, "as the photo is fairly old and the house does not look like that anymore, but the person in the back looks like someone I recall, and I think I know where this might be."

I leaned forward and said, "You think you know where this is?" My heart was racing. I was feeling closer and closer to realizing my goal. With a reassuring nod, he said he was quite certain he knew where this house was. I gulped my tea, even though it was very hot, because I needed to get moving.

After we finished our tea, we got up and made our way to the vehicle. I was ecstatic and walked briskly ahead of everyone before turning around and realizing that they were casually strolling. Everything had changed in a matter of minutes. However, if you consider the time frame, almost ninety years had passed, so a few extra minutes were not going to make a difference. Still, that did not matter to me—I just needed to be there now!

This elder got into the front seat with Raja and Tony and pointed forward. He turned to us and said that the house was up this way, and with that, we were driving through the village. We went past various houses and I kept thinking, *Is it that one or that one?* but we just kept driving.

Finally, we pulled up in front of a cement house with archways and a veranda. No one was around. The elder and Raja asked for my photo and they both approached the house. Someone came out from the side of the house and they had a conversation. Every so often they would look at us, nod a bit, and look closer at the photo, and then I got the look that I was not hoping for: a shake of the head to indicate "no." I sank a bit in my seat, but then more people gathered and looked at the photo. One person in particular seemed to be motioning more than the others, and the elder was interested in what he was saying. It was like watching a silent movie. This person in a white kurta now got into the four-by-four and the elder joined us in the back seat. As we were about to depart, we opened our window and gave out more of our sweets to the people around the area.

Turns out that Jandoli is divided into two parts, a new part, where we were, and the old part, where we were headed. We drove for a little while and the bigger concrete houses started to give way to more rustic, older dwellings. The sides of the roads were more dusty and weathered. There was a sense of community here, with people seeming to know each other, and as we drove by, people would wave to the elder and the person next to Raja. The elder appeared to be enjoying the attention and the sense that he was helping us fulfill a mission. Children playing along the side of the road would chase after our truck, because we were moving very slowly. Eventually, we pulled over to the side of the road because the person in the front seat was motioning to a location. I looked at the photo and nothing seemed to remotely resemble this area, but that could just be because so much time had passed.

Sadhna and I stayed in the vehicle as everyone else walked over to a couple of people under a tree. Again, there was a conversation, motioning back to us, and showing of the photograph, and then a few other people started to gather around the core group. There was some head shaking and the photo was passed along. Once again, one person seemed to be more prominent in the conversation and very adamant that he knew where this house was. He pointed down the road and told Raja that you go a bit this way, go right, then a bit this way, and you will come to a well, go this way, and so forth. Raja was nodding and we could overhear the conversation: "The person in the back [in the photograph] is so-and-so and their house is that way!"

We dropped off the person we had picked up at this place and a new traveller joined us, who said he had a strong idea that the house belonged to a family he knew in the village. We left more sweets there as a sign of gratitude and the children all came running up to us to have some. There was only one box left.

We continued driving, and it felt as if I was lost in a maze as we went past the well, went one way and then another, and then seemed to double back. Eventually, we pulled up to a house with a high concrete wall. Again, Raja and the others got out and walked up to the house. A person was working in their small patch of garden and stopped when they saw us. They knew the elder, and exchanged pleasantries. They looked at the photo and over to us, and I could tell there was no excitement or assurance this time. Our search had ended at this point.

My heart sank. We did not have a glimmer of hope of finding the house or my family. Slowly, the dream of connecting with my roots was withering. Like a candle at the end of its wick, the flame burned less and less bright, and then, with one last flicker, it went out in a puff of smoke. We left our last box of sweets with this family and, shoulders slumped, drove back in silence to drop off the elder. He too seemed disappointed, as he had really wanted to help. While driving back, I opened my journal and wrote: "Today we struck out!!!"

Everyone had their own thoughts at this point, but what I was feeling was dejection and sadness. Maybe people were right after all, and I had taken on a challenge that was too difficult or too big.

Within a few minutes we pulled into the courtyard where we had started, and once more we all got out. The family came up to us with smiles, but when they saw our faces, the smiles turned to concern. Comforting us, they said, "While you could not find your village and home, please come back tomorrow and become part of our family. We would be happy to host you, and you can enjoy a nice family meal with us." It was an authentic gesture of hospitality. We took the elder's phone number and said we would have to rearrange our plans and consider options, and we might take them up on their offer. With hugs and smiles, they wished us well. Jandoli may have been the wrong village, but we had met wonderful people.

I might not have found my roots, but I had discovered something else. I realized how genuine, warm, and considerate people can be. These folks had just met us, and now they wanted to open their house to us and welcome us into their family.

It was now early evening and the drive back to the hotel was quieter and felt longer. Raja turned on the radio to some classical Indian tunes to try to lighten the mood. No one talked and I was reflecting on the day of eagerness and disappointment, and the peaks and valleys that we had encountered. We tried and we came up short. I did not have a plan for the following day, because I had gone in thinking confidently that we would find the house and that tomorrow we would return as heroes to a welcome and a triumphant gathering of the reunited generations. Instead, I was left with a photograph and really nothing more.

I had attached myself to something that I knew was not going to be easy but was also not impossible. It was a SMART goal: Specific, Measurable, Attainable, Relevant, and Timely. I had done my research and follow-up, and spoken to people from the area. I knew it would be difficult to accomplish, but a small part of me was optimistic. How amazing would it have been to find a lost part of our family. I now reconciled myself to the knowledge that coming to the district but not finding the house was as close as I could get to my roots.

Sometimes we set an objective knowing it to be an ambitious goal. We need to be comfortable in accepting that we may not accomplish all that we set out to do but that we might have valuable experiences in the process. I had not listened to the noise, and had pursued what I needed to do. I personally felt lost where my identity was concerned, and I had found it in the Golden Temple. I needed to accept that this trip was not a total loss and that I would carry memories with me for the rest of my life. Sure, the search was a huge part of the trip, but sometimes we must turn around and tell ourselves, "I will be better prepared the next time I make a trip out this way, and then I will find it." I told myself I would make a return journey. I would not give up.

A failure is where you try something, it does not work, and you give up. I thought some might consider this a fail; I chose to call it a setback. It made me stronger as a person and more resilient.

20

IF AT FIRST YOU DON'T DON'T SUCCEED...

Chodauri?

HAVING ARRIVED BACK at the hotel, I made my way to the room, took off the tunic, and tossed it on a chair. I plopped on the bed as the day finally caught up to me. I closed my eyes, thinking that somewhere out there were the village and someone who was a link to my past. I could sense it. I was close, but not close enough. I considered what was next, but first I had to call home, because they were anxiously awaiting news of our search.

My mother answered the phone and was happy to hear my voice. After the exchange and updates about food and shopping and sightseeing, I asked if Dad was there. When Dad came on, all I could muster was, "I tried, but it did not work out." He said, "That is all right.

You tried and you have put great effort and work into this. As long as you are enjoying yourself, that is all that matters." He said it with genuine sincerity. I appreciated his words; however, the sentiment did not seem to resonate with me. Finding the village was important to me and to him.

There was more conversation and I was on autopilot, sharing the journey to the Punjab and what it was like at the Golden Temple, but a part of me was also thinking, *What is next? Maybe I should try a different approach. Can I give up this easily? I am here and have one more day, so maybe we should try again but from a different angle.* I was feeling a renewed sense of urgency; I did not want to give up after just one attempt. I had less than twenty-four hours before Raja would have to return us to Delhi, as that is what we had agreed upon and he had another commitment. It felt as though the clock was working against me. We could have devoted more time to finding the village, but we had purposely limited our quest to two full days so we could also experience other aspects of India. Plus, we had carefully booked our time frame, hotels, and drivers; it would be too difficult to change it all this late in the game. At this point, I had used up whatever information I had. We ended our call with my dad saying, "Enjoy the rest of your trip and don't worry, you did your best." I smiled. I don't think he knew that I was not going to give up just like that.

I pulled out the map and looked at it carefully. Sadhna felt that we had tried and it hadn't worked, so tomorrow we should explore Jalandhar and the area around it.

Her view was that perhaps shopping would be a great distraction from today, and she made it sound as if we would be doing it for me. I did not say anything, but inside I was scheming. I had different plans for tomorrow, but I needed Raja's approval on this and would have to wait until tomorrow morning to tell Sadhna. One more attempt was mounting inside me.

I got up early the next day. At breakfast, I told Sadhna that I wanted to try again. "Forget what everyone has told us," I said. "Let's just go to Garhshankar and ask around, show them the photo, go back to basics." My thought was that maybe Jandoli was the wrong village after all, and perhaps someone in Garhshankar had heard of Chodauri. I could sense a bit of disappointment in Sadhna, but there would be ample time for shopping throughout the remainder of our trip.

Raja arrived at the hotel and I could see that he too was disappointed that we hadn't found the village. Before I could say anything, he said he would like to try again today. I told him my Hail Mary plan, and he nodded in agreement. We probably had about ten hours to find the village, as the next day we would be heading back to Delhi. We got into the truck and were off, with my map, journal, photograph, and hope along for the ride. "Determination" summed up the moment: I was determined to find the village, and Raja was determined to help reunite the past to the present in any way he could.

The drive to Garhshankar seemed to go by more quickly this time. We pulled over in a fairly busy part of the town and Raja got out. He went up to one person after another and showed them the photo. The people would look at it, look over to us, look back at the photo, and then shake their head no. Slowly, my enthusiasm started to dissipate. I took a deep breath, but Raja was not willing to give up. Like a child looking for a lost puppy, he was walking about with the photo in his hand and asking people at random. I appreciated his persistence.

As I was slipping into my own thoughts, I heard something that made me sit up abruptly: "*Chodauri or passé gay ha.*" (Yes, Chodauri is that way.) I saw a man pointing. From my rough understanding of Punjabi and Hindi, he was saying it was a village a few kilometres up this side road. I was reserved but slightly enthusiastic. Could this really be happening? Had I heard correctly, or was I mistaken? No, this person seemed insistent that Chodauri was this direction. He stood to the side of the truck and smiled, saying he was willing to help. The man stroked his beard as he gave Raja directions to the village. We thanked him, saluted, and were off again.

I now understood why Chodauri had been so difficult to find. We had been told that when my grandfather asked for letters to be written to the village, it was in the district of Hoshiarpur. Well, the district that we were directed towards was Nawanshahr, which means "new town." It was established in 1995, and Chodauri went from being in Hoshiarpur to Nawanshahr when the district boundaries were redrawn. So it was clear why the village had been elusive: we had been looking in the wrong district!

Fifteen or twenty minutes passed as we drove along a rural road. We approached a brick archway at the road-side. Seated there, cross-legged and with arms folded, was a thin old man who looked as though he had fallen off a charm bracelet. He was wearing a scruffy turban and had on a faded cream-coloured shalwar, a colour-ful sweater vest, and dress shoes with no socks. His thin face and scruffy beard showed someone who had worked the land in his time, and he was hunched over, looking at a patch of ground, deep in thought. *Not a con-vincing sentry*, I thought. Raja pulled over because he wondered if this person might tell us where Chodauri was. It was now 2 p.m. and our turnaround time was nearing; just three more hours and we would have to call this whole thing off. Raja went to speak to the man, and I heard the words, *"Chodauri et tey ha."* (Chodauri is here!) The man pointed through the archway to a side road and began looking up at us. *What! We are at Cho-dauri?* Excitement started to rise and I sat up.

I asked in my broken Hindi, *"Uncle, yeh Chodauri hai?"* (This is Chodauri?) I wanted reassurance. Part of me longed to believe that this was truly Chodauri, but another part was reserved, thinking that perhaps this was like "Jandoli" and only sounded like "Chodauri." Being here did not mean it was our village.

The old man took the photo from Raja and studied it carefully, as everyone else had done. He squinted and brought it closer for inspection. I was a bit skeptical that he could make out anyone because he was so elderly, he had no glasses on, and the photo was not very clear to begin with. He tapped one person. He didn't know the house, but he said one person in the picture looked like so-and-so, and their house was up the road. Once again the obscure image of the old man in the back was identified as the connecting link. I was thinking, *Here we go again*, and like a movie replayed, the old man put his hands on his knees and slowly rose, got into our truck, and pointed forward. Charge!

21

... TRY,
TRY AGAIN

Chhaduari

THE OLD MAN sat in the front seat, giving directions. We drove for a short while and there were some homes and some random people sitting and walking. It reminded me of Jandoli. After a few minutes, the old man held up the photo and pointed to a house that was approaching on our left. It did not look anything like the house in the photograph, but I expected that was because it was an old photo.

We pulled over and the old man got out and so did we. I looked around. There was a driveway leading up to a house. Next to it was an open pen and a couple of water buffalo lounging about, chewing their cud. They glanced our way and, not very interested in what was going on, went back to what they were doing. Across the road was a big open field where the soil had been prepared and mustard plants grew in abundance. I thought that this place could be anywhere in India, as there was nothing unique about it. For all I knew, we could have been back in Jandoli, because there were no distinct markers.

The old man and Raja proceeded up the driveway at a quick pace. The old man was hunched over, arms swinging, his bowed legs carrying him smoothly, with us a few steps behind. The house was being constructed and it was difficult to tell if it was a renovation or new. The courtyard was an open space and there were green tiles laid out that led to the house. Along the side was a concrete wall with archways that guided us along.

I guess a couple of people inside the house saw us, because they came outside. They knew the old man and exchanged pleasantries. As Raja and the old man consulted with the three or four people standing there, they looked towards us and heard the story while the old man showed them the photo. We were about ten or fifteen feet back and could make out the Punjabi language to some extent. The people from inside the house studied the photo. One old lady, wearing a green Indian suit and a blue jumper, was adjusting her white *chunni* (scarf) and her glasses. She looked carefully at the photo and I heard her say, "*Mah ha! Mah photo vich ah!*" (That's me! That's me in the photo!)

I stood there with my eyes wide and held my breath. She looked over to me and I looked back at her. Did I hear things correctly? My Hindi and Punjabi were not great, but I was pretty sure I'd understood what she'd said. She held the photo and wanted to know who we were and how we came to possess this photo. I moved forward and, with Raja's help, explained in Hindi that I had come from Canada and that I was looking for the house of my grandfather, Labh Singh. She stood there for a moment in surprise and kept studying us. I was not sure if this was a good thing, because I was not 100 percent certain that this was the right place, and I had been warned we might not get a warm reception. I didn't know if I was really prepared for a negative response.

We continued to look at each other, and then suddenly she walked up to me, hugged me, and said, "You are home." She had tears in her eyes and this caused me to weep as well. We hugged for a while and I closed my eyes.

My journey was over. I had found my grandfather's house. I had found the needle in the haystack even though we did not even know the haystack was!

I felt a blend of emotions: joy, sadness, excitement, and triumph. The sadness surprised me, but I think it was because I realized we had had a long separation and they knew very little about us and we knew very little about them. Our lives had been parallel but we were unknown to one another, until this moment when I had brought the two strands together. We could communicate and had some commonality, but we came from different worlds. There were many people who had passed away and whom we would never know. Equally, they were not going to leave the village to come home with us and learn about our lives. We were on separate banks of a divide, with only a tenuous bridge connecting us. We could see them and they could see us, and the bridge would have to be our contact point.

She held my hand and we walked up the driveway together to the house. We had only just barely scratched the surface of who we were and why we were here. All we knew was that we belonged here and it was my village and these were my people. This was the place from where generations of my ancestors had emerged.

I had forgotten that there were other people present, and before I knew it, they were gathered around and hugging us. They knew we were family from far away and that was all we needed to know; it did not matter how we were related. The people who had said we would get a bad reception or they might not really care about the family ties were all wrong. The lady motioned to the younger people with haste to get some chairs from inside, and as the chairs started to appear, she invited us to sit.

Seated, I looked around for the old man who had got us to this place. I wanted to thank him, but I could not see him. Perhaps, satisfied that he had done a great deed today, he had disappeared into the village landscape, maybe back to his sentry post at the entrance to the village. He was our link to the past, and I am not sure we would have succeeded were it not for the person in Garhshankar and this man seated by the archway. There seemed to be some sort of cosmic intervention at work.

Now that we were seated, I found out that Parita Kaur* was the elder. She wanted to know more about

---

* names have been changed to protect privacy.

who we were. I explained that we came from Canada and that I was Labh Singh's grandson. I knew she was related to me because she asked if I was the son of Ranjit, my dad's older brother. I said I was the son of Jagjit, and she knew immediately who I was. When Ranjit had come by over twenty years ago, he had brought them up to date on who we all were. They had filled in the blanks on the family tree on this side but had never actually met anyone except Ranjit and his family.

As we sat in the courtyard, Parita held my hand. Her touch was soft and comforting. It was as if she had found something she had lost many years ago and did not want to let it go. Two of the people who were with Parita emerged to have tea with us. It was a rich, sweet, thick tea. I am not sure if it was the tea or the satisfaction of finding the village, but I sat there in total comfort. I learned that the reason the tea was so rich was that it was made with buffalo milk, courtesy of the two bovines that had shown so little interest in us. I savoured every drop.

After a few minutes, I saw others approaching the driveway at a brisk pace. It turned out that one of the younger people who was present when we first arrived had taken off to call her father, telling him that foreign guests had just arrived. I think she had filled him in on who we were, because he came up the driveway with a determined stride and a large smile. As he got closer, I stood up and he hugged me with a crushing force and, in Punjabi, welcomed us. We hugged for a while before he loosened his grip and introduced himself as Ketan Singh. I wanted to know more about him because it seemed he was the man of the house. When we separated, we both just looked at each other. He was a stout man who seemed solid in stature, and he resembled Labh in the photos I had seen. He had a salty grey beard and appeared to be about my age. His smile was genuine and warm, and his eyes crinkled at the corners as we talked and shared.

More and more people started coming up the driveway, wanting to hear who had appeared. The news of our arrival was spreading through the village and breaking up the daily routine.

As we sat by the front of the house, the kitchen started up. People were running about and wanting to look after us. Another round of tea arrived. I pulled out a mini photo album I had carried with me on the remote chance we would find the village. Parita and Ketan looked at the images with great care, and I described who the people were. When we came to a photo of my father's older brother, Ranjit, Parita put her finger on the page. She said, "I know him," and said in Hindi, "That's Ranjit. He never came back. How is he?"

I stopped and looked at her. I realized that with the loss of connection, no one had relayed the news of Ranjit's passing. I had to explain to Parita that Ranjit had passed away about twenty years ago, and now I had to relive that moment. It impacted me because Ranjit Singh had been a favourite uncle of mine. She went silent, took the album and looked at the picture, put her fingers on his image, and closed her eyes in thought. After a few moments she opened them and went to the next page. This was one of the confirmations that I was among family.

We found it! The house and family I thought I had lost. You can see Parita in the middle with her white scarf covering her head, and Ketan to her left and in front of me.

We had been warned to be careful, that people might dupe us for money. The fact that Parita knew my uncle was a confirmation, but not one I needed. I already knew I was among family. From the moment we met, there was no question in my mind.

Ketan said, "Let's take a walk and show you around a bit while the kitchen is busy." So walk we did. We went down the driveway and into the heart of the village. He pointed out some houses and places that were within the family confines but also many others. We walked through alleyways and saw various concrete houses.

The homes we walked past were modest in nature: two floors, white or some dull colour. They were scattered about as if someone had thrown a handful of dice into the air and wherever they landed, a house was built. The alleyways meandered between these structures. Some of the homes were worn down while others were newer. Out of the maze of pathways we came into an open space with a large tree in the middle that played the role of village centre. While Ketan explained aspects of village life, I took it in.

Children played with simple homemade toys, like paper kites. There was a ball being kicked around that was desperately in need of a pump, because it landed with a stationary thud. I saw conservatively dressed women in traditional Indian suits doing their household tasks, including hanging up the family laundry, sweeping, and chopping vegetables for dinner.

Some old men were sitting together under the tree. They were relaxing on wooden-framed beds and mattresses made of coiled and tightly woven rope. As they lounged about, they smoked a hookah (water pipe). Children dashed around them, and it made me smile: an intergenerational daycare. Now this was a community! It did not seem as though people worked independently of each other; there was a communal feeling to this village, and everyone had a part to play. Everything seemed connected and intertwined. For example, the elders were enjoying the day and the hookah, but they were also playing an integral role by managing the kids while the parents worked. The elders remained connected to the young, and the children were protected. The elders would glance about every so often like mother hens counting their brood.

This was where my grandfather had walked as a boy, unaware of the life and adventures and people ahead of him. What led him to decide to leave? Had he done something wrong and felt he needed to escape? Was it a sense of being confined and wanting to explore, or just a need to take a step and see how far he could go? From this village, he'd ventured out one night and headed to a faraway land that he knew nothing about. At that time, once you left, you were gone. I could only imagine what his parents went through when their adolescent son up and left. I understood he wrote to the village, but letters are merely a stamp of time—sort of like when we look up at the stars and see flickers. Those lights in the sky are only the remnants of the past.

I wondered what life was like back in the late 1800s. I'm sure families milled about much as they do today.

Core family values endure for generations, while the physical appearance of a village might not. It seemed that this village had progressed slowly, unlike the rapid change we're familiar with back in Canada. Even so, cellphones being pulled from pockets is a sight all too common from my world. However, it seemed that here, technology supplemented without fully penetrating village life; families were not sitting about checking their phones continually.

As I walked along the alleyways, I touched some of the buildings and trees. While the homes were obviously more recent than my grandfather's time, the trees had likely been here when he was young. Did he run around these trees with his friends?

I think I inherited my grandfather's tendency to explore and be curious. I have never settled on the easy and comfortable; I always venture out to learn about the world and myself. I leap when the world tells me to stay in one place. I want to know what is on the other side of the fence or wall. This is why I had taken on this adventure in the first place. Part of it was curiosity, and the other part was to prove to myself that I could accomplish what I set out to do. While I may not have known my grandfather, I felt a greater connection to him as a result of walking in his footsteps.

We went to one house and there were stairs leading to the rooftop. Ketan mentioned that this house belonged to one of our cousins. The words "one of our cousins" rang out. I was part of this community even though I had never been here before. We had been accepted. I was glad I had not listened to the people who could have deterred me from my journey to find my ancestral home. It got me thinking about the whole issue of family. While blood and DNA are one way to define a family, it is also much deeper than that. For me, family is about a personal way that we include people in our lives. That is why, when we run into an elder in Indian culture, we refer to them as auntie or uncle, or call someone our own age brother or sister. One might think that those words are used casually, but for me they are significant and are as true as if applied to blood relatives. Family is about how we create a sense of belonging and association with others. The people around us, connected to us by blood or by social lines, help us to form our own foundations and identity. To me, everyone is unique and special, and if we form a bond, we are family.

I appreciated how everything was open in our village, and it did not matter if this was your house or not, you could just make your way to the roof and no one would say anything. From the roof, I got a view of the houses in the area. This village was no small place. When the word "village" was used back home, I had imagined a small community of a hundred or so people. I could now see that the population was at least ten times that.

There were many houses and families in the area. I could see other rooftop balconies, open courtyards, and walled compounds. There were tables and chairs on the roofs of many homes, and this told me that families would gather on top of the houses and catch up on their daily activities. We stood there for a while. I wondered, with such a large village, how it was that no one had known where it was.

We hung out on the rooftop and talked for a bit. Ketan pointed around and shared with me that the village had a population of about a thousand. Many of the people here were also named Thiara, though a lot used the surname Singh. I had also wondered about that. Many people who had immigrated used a default name of Singh. When we were becoming Canadian citizens, the citizenship officer asked if we had a family name, as this would be a good transition point to switch it over. We found out through my uncle Ranjit that Thiara was the name, and we converted our legal documents accordingly.

We strolled back to the original house, where we found a late lunch being prepared. While I sat with Parita and Ketan, I had to ask about our family history. Who were these people before me? I only knew of my grandfather, but how did all the pieces fit? With pen in hand, I started to draw out the details as told to me by Parita and Ketan, and branches of my family tree started to appear.

Slowly, I could see the relationships start to connect and I could better appreciate and understand how I aligned to the village and how the village connected back to me. I learned about people and names that were foreign to me. I knew that my grandfather had an older brother, but I did not know his name, did not know if there were other siblings. I had no idea of uncles and cousins, and now I was in the presence of them all and taking this all in. With a flood of emotions, I wondered who they were. Without their knowing it, they all had a hand in who I was and where I had gone in life.

The two relations about whom I sat there wondering the most were my grandfather's two sisters that Ketan had told me about, Assi and Ruddi. They had married and left the village, as was customary. Where had their lives taken them? What family had transpired as a result?

Relationships can be so fragile and, if not cared for, can wither away. I sat there with my journal open in front of me and stared at what I had just written. This challenge was not just for me, but for my immediate family and extended family. I had captured the missing pieces of the puzzle that were hidden and almost lost. Now the picture was becoming clear.

On a piece of my journal paper, I started to draw out the relationships that I had just uncovered. My grandfather, Labh, had an older brother, Akal Singh. Akal had four sons, and the oldest one, Suman Singh, married Parita Kaur, and Ketan Singh was their son. It all started to make sense, and these faces now had a place in my journal.

We sat together and ate while many watched the "foreigners" enjoy the meal. They had quickly prepared an egg curry, vegetables, dahi (plain homemade yogurt), and roti. After I cleaned off my plate, I did what you should never do in an Indian household: I turned away from it to continue talking. While I chatted with some of the others who had arrived to learn about us, the cooks heaved more food onto my plate and looked at me with a loving satisfaction. I slowly ate and spoke, and now I was really taking my time. Then I picked up my plate and carried it over and said thank you.

I opened my book and took out my pen. I carefully wrote down our village address and phone number. This was a piece of information I did not want to lose. Ketan, watching as I wrote, said, "Chodauri," but spelled it *Chhaduari*. I looked at the lettering and showed it to him and he confirmed that it was spelled correctly. Part of the reason I had had such a difficult time finding the village was that its name was not passed along correctly.

Our family wanted us to stay the night, but we could not. We had to leave and get back to Jalandhar, because early next morning we were on our way to Delhi.

We had been in the village for three hours. From learning about our past to meeting new family, the time had gone by quickly. But there was one thing left for me to do. I reached into my side pockets and made sure they were still there. As Sadhna chatted with many of the guests, I asked Ketan to walk with me. We got up and went down the driveway to the road that had led us to the house. I stood there and looked out over the fields. I asked if this was "ours," and he said yes. We proceeded to walk out into the fields. I found a patch that was bare and reached into my pockets and pulled out zip-lock bags that I had carried with me from Vancouver. I bent down, opened the bags, and scooped up some dirt. The texture was dusty and fine. There were some clumps, but mostly it was a fine light-brown powder. I carefully placed the soil in the bag and sealed it with a slide of my fingers. I was taking a bit of the village home with me. While still bending down, I pinched a small bit of dirt, closed my eyes, and tightly held the granules between my fingers. The dirt was the treasure I was now going to take home; with it in my possession, my journey to India felt complete.

Earlier, I had shared that my father became a paraplegic when I was young and that I really wanted to do something for him. I knew he would never be able to make it to the village or see the house his father had left, so perhaps I could bring the village back to him in a small bag. This soil was from our roots, his father's house. Without knowing the backstory, an onlooker would regard this as just dirt. But it is the significance of the dirt that makes it a treasure to me and my family. This treasure could not be bought; it was earned with persistence, and by overcoming noise and obstacles. This dirt was now one of our family riches.

We walked back to the house and everyone stood up. Parita grabbed my hand and asked if we would not stay. She said that after all these years, it was nice to have family back again. I thanked her and hugged her. Parita had tears in her eyes and she wiped them with her shawl. My eyes were misty as well. She was elderly and I was not sure if I would ever make a trip back to India or the village. She was my main link to the past. It reminded me how fragile this link really was. If she had not been here, would anyone in the house have recognized her in the photo? I also had a sense that, given her age, I might never see her again.

Ketan gave me a big, crushing hug. He told me to come back and that there would always be an open door for us. I quietly looked around at everyone, and then a flood of people came forward to hug us and say goodbye.

As we got into our SUV, I looked back one more time to see all these people waving. We started to drive away, and then the house and family were gone. We drove through the village, past the brick archway, where the sentry no longer sat, and were back on the road to Jalandhar. I felt as though I had conquered Everest. I have to admit that part of me was pleased that it had been a difficult struggle. At times we are confronted by hurdles and you must choose whether to face the challenge or not even try. If it had been as easy as getting off a plane, finding the village on a map, and going there, the story would not have been as interesting. This had been a difficult struggle, and the prize certainly was sweet.

We got back to the hotel about 9 p.m. I dropped my backpack and made the call home. As the line crackled, my father picked up the phone. He asked how we were, and I said, "I found it. I found our village!" The line went silent for a moment, and then my father replied, "What? You found it!" I could hear his jubilation, and he called out to Mom and told her we had been successful. Other family members gathered around and wanted to know who were they, how did they react, what did they say? My parents wanted to know it all, so I got to live it all over again. The fact that we were now able to trace our roots meant a lot to the family.

Tomorrow we would head back to Delhi. It was going to be a long day, but I felt triumphant in what had been accomplished. I went to bed satisfied.

While we were learning about our village, Ketan and a few others took me on a walking tour of Chhaduari. To be in the place where my grandfather walked as a child was a surreal moment for me.

22

MOVING
ON

I GOT UP EARLY, feeling as if I was in a dream state. Had I really accomplished what I had set out to do? It was a journey to discover my roots and seek out my village of Chhaduari (now spelled correctly!). Yes, it now felt like my village too, and not just because my grandfather was from there. Prior to our trip, Chhaduari was a place I'd heard of, but it wasn't truly mine; it was as though it didn't really exist. By finding it, I had created a connection to it. I felt happiness about the reunion, sadness upon leaving, relief that I had found what I was looking for, and a sense of contentment that I was able to connect two sides of a puzzle with the missing piece.

My sense of feeling like a foreigner partially melted away. I was still a foreigner, but now I felt I also belonged to this country and was connected to it. I chose to dress in a beige-coloured Indian tunic as a way to signify my change. I opened my journal to the pages that outlined family members we had lost. These were my people and this was my distant home. Prior to finding the house, I was only living in the world of possibility and hope. Now that I had found the village, I could claim myself as Indian and add a flavour to the kitchari mix I already was. I was a blend of flavours. Whereas before I had tried to fit in, now I truly did fit in. I was proud to be a hybrid Indian.

I had accomplished the three things I was hoping to do in India: visit the Taj Mahal, pay my respects at the Golden Temple, and seek out my village. Now we were heading back to Delhi to begin our final week. Fortunately, we had decided to make our last week more about easing the pace and experiencing the area and people. We would check back in to the Ambassador Hotel in Delhi, then take a train to Jaipur to explore the area. We had not booked a tour operator but felt we would be able to pick something up when we arrived there. I was more confident now about being in India, so maybe it was time to take off the training wheels and experience it on our own. After a day or two in Jaipur, we would head to Udaipur, which is farther south, and stay at one of the posh hotels in the area. Sadhna was looking forward to this as it was the style she had been hoping to experience. To this point, all of our hotels in India had been very nice, with the exception of the Janpath, but the Lake Palace Hotel in Udaipur seemed truly elegant as the photos showed it sitting in the middle of a massive lake and one had to take a boat to reach it.

In the end, I was still a foreigner, and perhaps I would never be accepted as a local, but the fact that I was able to create a link to my identity and past was an epic moment and one that could never be taken away. How had everything lined up and come together? Had there been some guiding force supporting me along the way? Was there a divine intervention of ancestors on the sidelines encouraging me along? I now had a great story that was worth sharing with my family, friends, and strangers. I felt there might be others searching for their past and my story might allow them a level of hope.

Instead of trying to push away an identity, I learned to embrace it as a valuable part of what makes me unique and complete. I found myself, and understood that I had never really been lost. My identity was within me; it just needed to be realized and awoken.

WITH A FINAL handshake, we said goodbye to our driver and walked into the international departures area. With the sliding doors closing behind us, we entered a familiar environment. In the beginning, when we arrived in India, the sliding doors had opened the world to us as foreigners. Now we walked through another set of sliding doors that would begin our journey back to Canada, but I didn't feel the same. A significant transformation had occurred.

I was not looking forward to the twenty-four hours of travel that lay before us. As I stepped towards the

Air Canada desk, an Indian representative of the airline smiled at me. She was a lovely Indian woman with long braided hair, a red bindi dot on her forehead, and an Air Canada uniform. I was amused that her look was kitchari of sorts, a blend of India and Canada. We struck up a conversation with her and relayed our story, and she was most impressed by it and called out to her manager. We shared our story with him as well, and he was moved by it. Then we made our way through the security area to our departure gate, where we patiently waited for our flight.

As I thumbed through my travel journal, a PA announcement came on and asked us to approach the desk. As we walked up, the manager smiled and said that he had really appreciated our story, and that he had some good news and some bad news for us. "What is the good news?" I asked. He said they had a couple of seats in first class and we would be upgraded. Excited, I accepted, but then, with hesitation, I asked, "But you said there was also bad news." He said, "Yes, unfortunately, they are not together." To which I replied, "So what is the bad news?" At which Sadhna just rolled her eyes, sighed, and looked to the ceiling while I smiled at the manager.

Waiting for our flight, I reflected. I had arrived with the word "uncertainty" prominent in my mind, and now it had been replaced by "certainty." I had a better appreciation and understanding of who I was. Did India feel like another home to me? I would say that while I felt a connection to India ethnically, culturally, and spiritually,

TOP At the tail end of the trip, we stopped at Udaipur and the beautiful Lake Palace Hotel. I was no longer a tourist, foreigner or local—I was kitchari and grateful for this identity that the trip had created in me. I found the past and I found myself.

BOTTOM My prized upgraded boarding pass that took me home to Canada.

I was still foreign to this place. Looking down at the *kara* on my right wrist and rubbing it between the fingers of my left hand, it dawned on me that instead of trying to say I am now Indian, my realization was that I had always been Indian. I just needed to expose myself to the experiences that would unlock my Indian identity.

EPILOGUE

WE PULLED INTO the driveway of my parents' home and prepared for a reunion. Family came out to see us and we got our customary hugs. As we went in, the kettle was put on and we sat around the table and relived our adventures.

I opened my backpack and took out ten pounds of Indian sweets, just the right ingredient to have with our tea and stories. I then reached inside again and pulled out a little Tupperware container that protected the zip-lock bags and handed it to my father, who did not know what was inside. He opened the container and pulled out a bag. I explained how this was the soil from our village and that it was for him. Tears welled up in our eyes as he opened it and pinched a bit between his fingers. My father had never been to the village, but the village was brought back to him.

To some it is just soil from a little village in India, but to me this is
treasure—the ground where my ancestors walked.

The phone began to ring as aunts and uncles called to hear our voices. The doorbell rang and more family came by, and as they joined us for tea and sweets, Sadhna told stories of her shopping adventures and our temple visits. As for me, the day before I left India, my mom had asked me on the phone what I felt like eating for my first meal back in Canada. She does this every time I travel. Of course, this time I said, "Kitchari!" I now took a plate of it and walked out onto the sundeck. I sat outside in the cold and looked up to the clear sky. The stars were out and I could see the crescent moon. I thought, *India is just on the other side of the world, and we share the same moon.* Prior to the journey, it had felt as though India was in another galaxy, but now it didn't seem so distant after all.

YOU ARE
A JOURNEY.

YOU CREATE
MEMORIES.

YOU ARE
A STORY
WAITING
TO BE TOLD.

REFLECTION
QUESTIONS

1 We each have a unique background. I am a British-born Canadian with parents from Fiji and grandparents from India. Share what your background is. Are you kitchari, like me?

2 I found a spiritual home at the Golden Temple in Amritsar. Where have you found a spiritual home in your life? Where have you found a moment that provided you with calmness and peace? Was it a church, or a place in nature? Describe the feeling you had when you visited the place.

3 Going to India, I should not have been a foreigner, but I was—both in my self-perception and in how I was treated. Describe a place you have been to where you did not feel entirely comfortable. How did you

try to fit in? Did it work? What did you learn in the process?

4   I was persistent and relentless in my pursuit. Share a story about something that really mattered to you, or a goal you went after. Why did it matter? How did you tackle it? What was the result?

5   Where would you like to go for your next trip, and why would you choose to go there? How would you prepare for the trip?

6   For me, the soil from my village has become one of my most important treasures. Talk about an artifact you have that holds purpose and meaning. How did you come to possess it? Why is it important to you?

7   I did a TEDx talk about sharing stories, using a concept I came up with called CARPE. Take a moment and think of situations and times for each word, and describe what they mean to you.

   - **Curiosity**: We go through life with natural curiosity. What was the last thing you were curious about?

   - **Appreciation**: There is a need for us to appreciate things for more than what they are. What or whom do you appreciate, and why?

   - **Reflection**: Think deeply about everyday occurrences, and add purpose and meaning to them. Take something simple and see if you can add a different meaning to it. For example, an hour-glass is a vessel of time. Can you reflect on it and see how it also represents life?

- **Perspectives:** We each have perspectives. How have yours been shaped? Have you taken the time to identify what your perspectives are?

- **Experience:** Capture your stories and experiences so they are not lost. Share a story about your favourite vacation or something that happened to you when you were growing up.

ACKNOWLEDGEMENTS

I WISH TO THANK all the family members who not only provided me with the inspiration to pursue this journey but were also able to fill in some of the missing pieces that helped make the adventure possible. The trip was only accomplished by a collaborative and combined effort.

Thank you to all the individuals whom we met and who were part of our travels in India. They opened up their world and hearts so that I could better understand mine.

To all my friends and relations who have encouraged me to write this story. With a special note of thanks to my dear friend Mike Schauch because we both started writing our respective travel memoirs at the same time and supported each other through this challenging process.

Finally, to my wife, Sadhna, and our two boys, Ishaan and Sahil. Thanks to Sadhna for being on this adventure, and thanks to our two boys, who were not born when we travelled but who now have a better understanding of who they are as a result.

ABOUT
THE AUTHOR

S AM THIARA is a storyteller, writer, speaker, coach, work-shop facilitator, educator, and entrepreneur. He appreciates the opportunity to share and learn from his adventures, whether it is travelling to a far-off place or somewhere local.

Sam is the founder and Chief Motivating Officer at Ignite the Dream Coaching and Consulting, a platform that engages people to define their path. His goal is to engage individuals in their personal and professional development. For his work, he was recognized by the Governor General of Canada with the Canadian

Sovereign's Volunteer Medal and the Queen Elizabeth II Diamond Jubilee Medal. He was also a recipient of the Rick Hansen Difference Maker Medallion. Over the years, he has mentored hundreds, engaged thousands, and worked with more than forty-five non-profits.

He is a lecturer at the Beedie School of Business at Simon Fraser University, where he blends academic and professional experiences into a rich environment that captivates his audience. Sam's current area of expertise is engaging with post-secondary institutions, administrators, and educators so that the student's experience is at the centre. He also provides personal development to young professionals who are trying to better appreciate their journey. Equally, he is called upon to help with organizational alignment and improvements in companies.

An accomplished speaker, he has spoken at TEDx-SFU and TEDxLangaraCollege. Out of TEDxSFU, his first book emerged, *Personal Storytelling: Discovering the Extraordinary in the Ordinary*. He is sought after by conferences to share stories and his life experiences.

Everyone's life is an autobiography, make yours worth reading.
sam-thiara.com